Wild Ride

Women's Stories and Life Lessons by

Kathy Klaus, 55 Storytellers and You

Kathy Klaus

Kathy Klaus

RISE
PRESS

The Publisher: Rise Press is an imprint of Dragon Hill Publishing Ltd.

Library and Archives Canada Cataloguing in Publication
Title: Wild ride / Kathy Klaus.
Names: Klaus, Kathy, author.
Identifiers: Canadiana (print) 20210367547 | Canadiana (ebook) 20210367555 | ISBN 9781896124827 (softcover) | ISBN 9781896124834 (PDF)
Subjects: LCGFT: Short stories.
Classification: LCC PS8621.L383 W55 2022 | DDC C813/.6—dc23

Project Director: Marina Michaelides
Editor: Ashley Bilodeau
Designer: Tamara Hartson
Cover Image: Background painting by Kathy Klaus
          Wild Ride sculpture by Shelley Tincher Buonaiuto

The Stories: The stories in this book are the property of the Storytellers, and they retain all rights to their work.

Image Credits: Thanks to all the Storytellers for providing their own photos and and those of their loved ones.

Disclaimer: The information provided in this book is specifically designed for motivation and inspiration of its readers and should not be used as a substitute for professional counselling or therapy. This book contains the views and opinions of the author and the storytellers herein. Any action you take as a result of using this book is strictly at your own risk, and neither the publisher nor the author is liable for any damages, including psychological, physical, emotional, financial, commercial or incidental.

Produced with the assistance of the Government of Alberta.

Alberta Government

Printed in China

PC: 38-1

DEDICATION

Sages who nourish, cherish and entertain;

Freelancers who eulogize, strategize and materialize;

Wordsmiths who write crosswise on tiny scraps of paper;

Biographers who narrate, weblog, chronicle and journal;

the Columnist, Lyricist, Novelist, Memoirist;

And 55 Storytellers with the courage to recall, recount and share.

Contents

About This Book

These stories, arranged in random order, are divided into four sections—*The Value of a Story, Memories And Emotion, Gratitude* and *Love Remembered*. The topics explored in each section (like the keynote presentations at a writer's retreat) are elements that are common in all stories in this book.

Each submission, regardless of subject, length or being personally written or submitted by a family member, is paired with an image that illustrates each Storyteller's Wild Ride.

Woven throughout the book is a Writer's Retreat, inspired by the stories, with reading and writing exercises that can reflect upon the reader's own Wild Ride. It is recommended that the Writer's Retreat be savoured in small bites over a weekend, a month or beyond.

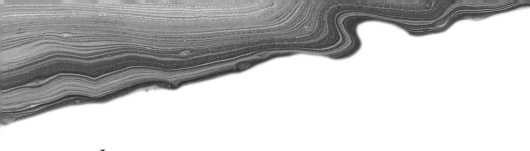

INTRODUCTION

Sculpture by
Shelley Tincher Buonaiuto

Wild Ride is a whimsical sculpture that, when added to a colourful sea of turbulence (as on the cover), simulates the ups, downs and arounds of a woman's life. I asked 55 women to share a story from any event or stage of their life—their Wild Ride. What I didn't expect was that the sharing of their stories would evolve into a unique experience, much like a writing retreat—surprising, unplanned, freshly imagined, all the qualities of a Wild Ride!

"…seeing she was so exuberant, she needed to be lifted to correspond with her spirits, so I put her on a flying carpet…"

–Shelley Tincher Buonaiuto, Sculptor

The *Wild Ride* sculpture was gifted to me years ago by my son, Daniel Klaus. At the time, my growing business provided a lot of stress—phones ringing nonstop, staff shortages and financial burdens.

My son and I were together on a rare excursion, window shopping at an appealing gift store in Austin, Texas. When Daniel saw the sculpture, he immediately became excited then made the purchase when my back was turned.

Later, when he gave it to me, he said, "Place this right beside your phone. If it doesn't put a smile on your face every time you see it, there's no hope for you."

The sculpture, and his constant support, has kept my spirits lifted and inspired me through the years.

WORDS TO LIVE BY

"Life should not be a journey to the grave with the intention of arriving safely in an attractive and well-preserved body, but rather to skid in sideways, body thoroughly used up, totally worn out, and screaming, 'Woohoo, what a ride!'"

–Hunter S. Thompson, *The Proud Highway*
Provided by Beverly Eanes

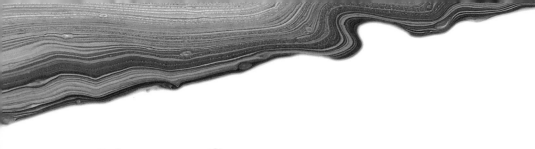

MEET AND GREET

We are all story...

Welcome everyone. Non-writers, some-time writers, experienced writers—anyone who is willing to recall a memory and write is a life and legacy hero.

I have a lifelong love affair with stories: the fish that jumped into the boat; the popcorn maker that caught on fire at the trade show; the priest's bowler hat, covered in fluff and fuzz that was finally found under the sofa.

In response to a project assignment at the Humor Academy, and inspired by a whimsical sculpture called *Wild Ride*, I invited women to share a memory from any event or stage of their life. I was thrilled and filled with gratitude to receive stories from 55 guest Storytellers who make up this book, *Wild Ride*. They cover a cornucopia of topics from city to farm, travels abroad and everyday family life. They are authentically heartfelt, funny, bold and inspiring. Some of their stories may resonate with you as the friend who is your cheerleader, the grandmother you miss or the sage you wished for.

The Surrounded by Story retreat component of this book is a reimagined view of what could be—a treasury of real-life stories combined with a self-worth shop, accessible no matter where you are. It was born from the realization that our lives are made of stories from which we can benefit when we more closely integrate them into our lives.

The art of remembering is a curious interplay of memory, emotion and science, continually being studied in an evolving field. When we recall stories, it is the emotionally charged memories that spring to mind immediately; frequently they can be traumatic events. Our positive memories often need to be coaxed.

This retreat focuses on nurturing our positive memories, the ones that we want to enjoy in the years to come. The key is balance: learning from the past allows us to fully live in the present and look forward to the future.

Four Keynote Presentations illuminate the relationship of story, memory, emotion and gratitude and provide the condensed results of research, personal account and commentary. Combined with the insightful stories from our guest Storytellers, each presentation ends with a Breakout Room that offers opportunities to record your own thoughts and emotions, and welcomes you to flow with your own story.

I invite you to pour yourself a cup of tea, a mug of coffee or a tumbler of cocoa, then settle into a deep and comfy space and sink into the stories. Allow each sincere voice to blend with yours and indulge in this, your own writing retreat. Make sure to write in the margins, doodle and loop your favourite word over and over. This book is your canvas now.

I'm excited by the potential of this journey. My heart urges you to feel welcome and find value as you navigate these pages. If I were with you, I would wrap your shoulders with a chenille throw and top up your beverage.

If you are new to writing and on the sweet side of forty, perhaps you will connect with a sage or two. If you are transitioning to your next adventure, the honesty in the advice the authors shared "with their younger selves" may bring clarity. If legacy becomes important, your own journaling could become the personal insight that will bring inspiration to a granddaughter.

From my heart to yours, I invite you to put aside the activity of busyness and gently fall into the soft spaces throughout… all the while surrounded by story.

Now that you have an idea of the retreat, let me introduce myself and then we can get into discovering the power of memories and the value of story.

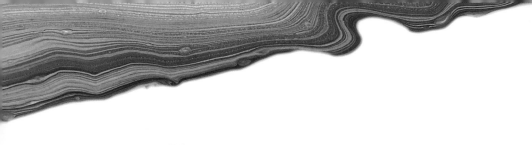

KATHY KLAUS

As a social worker, I am all about interactive activities and connection. But a move down under and a playful discovery changed the course of my life, and I took a surprising turn into business.

If you are under fifty and have, at some point, visited a doctor's office or airport, you might have experienced the popular bead and wire mazes— primary-coloured beads on twisting wires anchored into a smooth wooden base—designed and manufactured by Educo, the company I launched and ran for more than twenty-five years. The mazes became a classic early learning product and a staple in daycare, schools, doctor's offices and public spaces throughout the world.

Creating and running a successful business was an amazing period of my life; it was exhilarating to exhibit in annual trade fairs including Toronto, New York, Nuremberg, Dubai and Hong Kong and later establish channels of distribution.

The thrill of seeing our product for the first time in the iconic flagship store of FAO Schwarz Toys in New York is balanced by the pride of watching a child's moment of first discovery in a daycare setting in Japan. There were successes, near misses and clear misses and a curio cabinet of awards, but most importantly, experiences and friendships in far flung places. What a ride!

When I wanted fewer business responsibilities, my determination to forge a different path led me to selling the company. It was time to add more fun and a lightness to my life. I poured all my workshop knowledge in clowning and Laughter Yoga into volunteering at nursery schools and senior's residences. I joined The Association For Applied and Therapeutic Humor, and eventually enrolled in The Humor Academy. The experience helped me find the funny and recognize and appreciate the comedy that presents itself in everyday life. After three years of study, I was awarded the designation of Certified Humor Professional.

When asked to create a project as a second-year student, I applied my enduring interest in storytelling to the creation of *Wild Ride*—a natural choice. Collecting stories from 55 Storytellers was heartwarming and exciting. I didn't know then that it would lead to the expansion of the concept into this unique writer's retreat in a book.

In my toy design firm, our mission was guided by three principles: the concept had to be original or freshly reimagined, provide a safe learning experience and be breathtakingly beautiful. As my focus has turned to writing and storytelling, these tenets remain the same. I continue to be inspired by expert information, a safe place to share heartfelt stories and explore eye-catching graphics. Inspirational quotes rank highly, too.

Walking in nature with my Golden Retrievers, as well as looking for humour wherever it appears, provides daily laughter and inspiration. Connection and friendship are important to me. For more than two decades, I have not missed an annual women's salmon fishing derby. My husband, Larry, and I call Alberta, Canada, our home. We keep in close contact with our sons and grandchildren in New York.

The Value of a Story

With gratitude and through collaboration, I share authentic stories of humour and warmth to help others discover the storyteller in themselves.

– Kathy Klaus

Keynote: The Value of a Story

Highlights

- Storytelling is the oldest form of communication

- For maximum impact, embed your message in a story

- Family storytelling positively impacts children

- Elders' stories pass on family values and traditions

- Stories are not always fact

Every story is dependent on the perspective and memory of the Storyteller

Storytelling is the oldest of all art forms and pre-dates written language. I believe there is immense value in the shared stories of women. Created from every aspect of life, stories provide connection to our deeper selves and allow us to see and share the world around us.

There is no shelf life to a story. Think about the message in the songs we sing, the movies we watch, a schoolteacher's lesson and a salesperson's pitch. The most successful advertisers embed story to create powerful messages.

In families, sharing stories continues to be the favourite way for elders to pass on life lessons, values and traditions. Studies show the positive impacts that family storytelling has on a child's sense of self, social skills and ability to navigate life. I can tell my children how great-grandmother took pride growing vegetables, but there is nothing like a story to connect the emotions and life lessons that will be remembered for a lifetime.

Grandpa built a small greenhouse in the backyard for Grandma, who had a green thumb. Every morning she would get up early to run out and check on her tomatoes. She would turn the tomato plants to the sun, water them and often hum while working. In the afternoon she would go back to the greenhouse and choose the biggest, ripest, red tomato and bring it into the kitchen. She would slice it, and we would choose our own piece of tomato, place it on her homemade bread, then bite into the succulent tomato sandwiches that were so flavourful and delicious that the juice would drip off our chins.

North American Indigenous Peoples have been credited with the following philosophy:

Tell me a fact and I will learn. Tell me a truth and I will believe. But tell me a story, and it will live in my heart forever.

My four siblings and I were raised by the same parents, in the same home and in the same small community. And yet, when we gather and start comparing stories, our experiences are remarkably different. Research tells us that stories are not always fact. They depend entirely on the values, perspective and memory of the Storyteller.

Six-and-a-half-year-old Stevie knew from his mother's desperate reaction that he had crossed the line. He didn't know it would cause a fire, and he was sure his dad was going to be mad. Recalling the talk at school about how playmates had been spanked, in his panicked and fearful state, he ran to the garage to find one of those wooden things dad was putting on the roof. He tucked the small board down the back of his pants, just in case his Dad was really angry. When his dad heard the story and absorbed the danger that could have been, he had to catch his breath. When he saw the board sticking up above the little waistband, he had to turn his head away to hide his amusement; he placed his hand on Stevie's shoulder and marched him into the house for what promised, at the very least, to be, "the talk."

When Stevie grows up, I wonder how he and his parents will remember this story.

Comparing stories and listening to different points of view can heal families and patch misunderstandings of the past. When you understand why your dad sold his precious violin, why the kids were laughing at the skating rink, how a family event went so horribly wrong, it provides an opportunity to see things through someone else's eyes.

The stories we tell weave moments, days and years into a meaningful tapestry of our lives. The way we tell these stories is directly related to long-term well-being and resilience. Stories educate, entertain and create memories that endure.

Who doesn't love a good story?

Words To Live By

"So many versions of just one memory, and yet none of them were right or wrong. Instead, they were all pieces. Only when fitted together, edge to edge, could they even begin to tell the whole story."

–Sarah Dessen, *Just Listen*

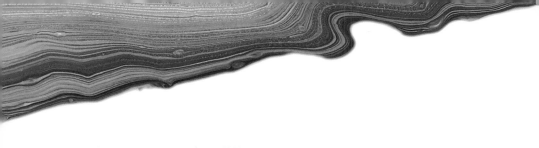

SURVIVAL AT HOME
Kathryn Holmes

Writing since grade school, Kathryn Holmes' first book, *I Stand with Courage: One Woman's Journey to Conquer Paralysis*, was not published until 2011, after being told she would be paralyzed from the waist down for the rest of her life. Several books later, and after her husband passed, she created *Thoughts and Prayers for Those Experiencing Loss*. Kathryn enjoys writing about faith, challenges and courage.

First my husband passed away, thus initiating me into the Widow's Club. Then the Coronavirus pandemic struck, and I became isolated from my family and friends. It was just my dog, Honey, and me. At the time of writing this, the world is still amid the pandemic; so far I have learned to recognize and be thankful for the simpler things that make my life a little more bearable.

In the morning I am greeted with a raspy tongue trying to exfoliate my face. She is persistent and tells me she loves me so much she nearly peels the skin off. That's true love.

Then I head to the bathroom and am welcomed with a flip of the lid from my toilet. Her name is Toto, and she's a Washlet. Her warm seat soothes my bottom. She is waiting to bathe my tush in warm water and then blow it dry. When I am away, I miss her.

I shiver as my walk-in tub fills with water. On with the jets to soothe my achy joints. Bubbles explode as I watch them inch toward the top of the tub. On two occasions, those innocent bubbles have overflowed onto the floor; I've become adept in catching them before they reach the rim. This is no small feat. After a half hour forcing the bubbles down, I wait as my tub empties. On with my day.

Breakfast comes in a box. In fact, so does lunch and dinner. I'm on a restricted calorie diet and am provided all my food. No mess, no fuss, no cooking. The food's not bad either.

Then Honey and I head out. She runs, pees, rolls in the grass, pees, chases squirrels, barks at other dogs, pees. Oops, poop, clean up. Aren't we having fun, mom?

Resting in my recliner in the sunroom, I start reading a book when, suddenly, there is a chill in the air. With a click I can turn on the fireplace without having to move my arthritic bones. If it's too hot, I can click on the fan. Too dark? Let there be light.

I miss my husband, but I can't say I miss his choice of television shows. No more football, soccer, tennis or any other sport. No more sappy sitcoms. I'm into the hard-core drama; it's so addictive I forget to go to bed.

Another day. Same routine.

Someday the world will be rid of the virus and we will all return to normal. Or is this normal?

ADVICE FOR MY YOUNGER SELF...

Don't worry about the future. You are stronger than you think. Enjoy each day.

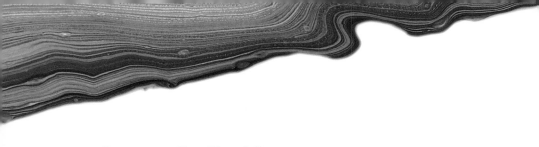

Queen Of Da Nile

Sharon McMullan-Baron

Sharon McMullan-Baron is an open-hearted creative who loves the arts, sciences and sports—and the people who engage in them. YOGA inspired, she instructs gentle classes of Hatha and Restorative Yoga.

In 2006, I was in the middle of chemotherapy for breast cancer. My husband and I were going to see a production of the Alberta Ballet. I was looking forward to the evening and seeing an old, dear friend, "P." He always lifted my spirits. I dressed with extra care, selected my wig and drew on my best eyebrows for the occasion.

Whenever I went to the Cross Cancer Institute, I visited The Wig Shoppe in the basement. The compassionate volunteers were fun as they helped patients select a wig to borrow. Over time, I chose over a dozen styles in all colors. I have fair skin and blue eyes, so the red wig gave me a mischievous air. The blonde wig garnered many smiles.

That evening, I pulled out a Cleopatra-inspired bob with straight black bangs. *Oh my, what a mysterious look,* I thought as I gazed into the mirror.

With my hand confidently hooked into my husband's elbow, I searched the Jubilee Auditorium's lobby for "P." We'd met in the boardroom of an arts organization years before. I trusted his opinion in matters of art, culture and fashion. He called it like he saw it. And he was always right. He and hubby smiled and shook hands. Then he turned to me. In the middle of our hug, he whispered, "Not this one."

"What?"

"No, my darling. Not this one. You are the Queen of many things...but not da Nile."

Our laughter exploded above the murmur of the crowd and the clinking of glasses.

I was in denial about my Cleopatra look! That wig went straight back to the Cross Cancer Institute basement. Once my hair grew back, I stayed with blonde locks. I have my hairdresser and "P" to thank for that.

WORDS TO LIVE BY

"You grow up the day you have your first real laugh at yourself."

–Ethel Barrymore, American Actor

A Wild Ride...Alberta Style
Lynn Gale

Poet, writer, yoga teacher and wellness advocate, Lynne Gale describes herself as grateful and a Libra, sun worshiper and earth goddess. An original member of the Tuesday Night Writers, her writing has appeared in anthologies through Stroll of Poets, Parkland Poets, Other Voices, Short-Edition and Chicken Soup for the Soul. Her poetry collection, *l'opacité*, was published in 2020.

A few years ago, my sister and I planned a birthday trip to Vancouver Island—a beach house for a week in July.

Day 1: Our flights arrive within minutes of each other. In our beautiful, classy green Mustang convertible, we're off to Victoria Harbor for an afternoon of whale-watching. It's cloudy but warm. Two hours later, we exit the cruise frozen and whale-less. It is raining; we crave warmth. Alas, our car's broken heater blows freezing air onto our icicle-encrusted bodies. We backtrack to the rental car place for a new, warm red convertible.

Day 2: Rainy and cold. We eat breakfast while wrapped in blankets. The waves pound the shore beneath angry clouds. We need to buy long pants and sweaters as well as Thelma and Louise style scarves to wear when the sun comes out, and we have the convertible roof down.

Days 3 and 4: Still raining. Ten degrees. Lots to see on the beach in the pouring rain. Back in Edmonton it's plus 25 degrees.

Day 5: Cloudy, cold, but no rain. A hike to Englishman River Falls presents a Groundhog Day challenge when we keep looping back to the same bridge no matter which way we go. Frozen again.

Day 6: Sunny and 12 degrees! Finally, a trip to Cathedral Grove with the roof down. We don our new scarves while laughing hysterically at ourselves—two crazy women in funny scarves in a red Mustang convertible singing at the top of their lungs to "Mamma Mia!" After ten minutes, our lips freeze, and we can barely hum. We stop to raise the roof but keep the scarves as our fingers are too cold to untie them. We need hot coffee.

Next trip, we'll come in November. It'll probably be warmer!

MY FAVOURITE QUOTE...

"Tell me, what else should I have done?

Doesn't everything die at last, and too soon?

Tell me, what is it you plan to do

With your one wild and precious life?"

–Mary Oliver

The Messenger

Karen Baxter

Passionate about empowering children to be kind, Karen Baxter creates volunteer opportunities that are a catalyst for a caring and connected community.

Tuesday November 7, 2017, may have been overcast, but spirits were high in the Baxter/Shoemaker households. Our daughter, Hayley, had been to the obstetrician the previous day. Her meltdown state and full-term pregnancy were indications to her doctor that an inducement should be scheduled. Today was the day!

It was my duty to deliver big brother Crue, our three-year-old grandson, to preschool. Upon his arrival, he jumped up and down announcing to all he had a baby!

"Not quite yet," I responded, laughing. Another Shoemaker baby was destined to be born today; in all probability the blessed event would take place in the evening.

My excitement over the course of the morning was just as high as it had been for the other grandchildren's arrival; undiminished because this was number three out of the chute. I knew it would be a long day!

Several years before, I had given my mom, Ruth, a glittering chickadee ornament for Christmas. It was a pretty little thing that adorned her bedside table and was aptly enjoyed by my bird-loving mom. Little did I know it would be featured prominently on this "birth" day.

When I picked Crue up from preschool later that morning, we had an intriguing encounter. As I opened a back door to my Nissan Rogue to help Crue into his car seat, he immediately exclaimed, "G (short for grandma), there's a bird in the car!"

Puzzled, but delighted with his imagination, I thought it must have been the topic of discussion in preschool that morning. However, my suspicious mind quickly took flight when I caught something fluttering in my peripheral vision! A screech of profanity escaped my vocal cords.

SHIIIITTTTTT!!!

Picture a bird in your car…I mean MY CAR!!!

My first inclination was to slam the door on Crue and this feathery terrorist. When faced with flight or fight, no contest! However, Crue, in typical three-year-old fashion, was completely unphased, so I couldn't assume the role of Scaredy Squirrel.

Hoping this unwelcome visitor would be only too happy to exit the vehicle, I quickly opened all the doors. However, feathery calmness reigned supreme, as it quietly perched on the dash. It observed me without panic, no sudden flutter or need to defecate from its nervousness. I can't say I felt the same. I could only assume it was injured. Reluctantly, I put on my mitten, gingerly picked it up then released it outside the car. Without a hint of injury, it flew off, aided, I'm sure, by the thrust from my adrenaline.

Afterward, I queried how the bird had entered the car. It was November. The windows had been closed, and the doors secured all morning, until I opened them to get Crue in. It had been waiting for us. It had to mean something, but what?

Two weeks later, as I was decorating for Christmas, I came across my mom's beloved chickadee ornament in one of my bins. I had retrieved it from her things after she passed. I was immediately struck with a moment of clarity and connection; the bird in the car had been a chickadee. My mom loved chickadees.

Its presence in the car that morning conveyed a wondrous message. Even though mom had passed seven years prior, her presence and love enveloped us that day, thanks to a sweet messenger.

As predicted, later that evening, beloved Monroe Patricia made her debut. I can't help but think she arrived securely encased in her great grandmother's love.

ADVICE FOR MY YOUNGER SELF...

As to what I would tell my younger self...never underestimate the power of a positive attitude, a sense of humour or a kind deed.

Fifty-year Friends
Roxanne Sumners

Roxanne Sumners lives and writes in Baja, California. She is guided by three Ah-has: Linear time is not real. We are infinite beings. We progress, despite appearances.

California, a November Saturday in 1967. I'm nineteen years old, and with my three best girlfriends, getting ready to go somewhere.

As I sit on Sharon's bed and watch her fuss with her makeup and hair, an indescribably wonderful feeling washes over, into and through me.

I'm just me, sitting there, but now it is as if I'm soaking and swaying in some strange, ethereal bliss.

I look around Sharon's room, sigh, rub my arms lightly and say, "I don't know what is happening to me, but something very strange is happening to me."

This moment is as clear now as it was then, over fifty years ago.

Oh! Now I remember! The four of us were going to The Pike. There was a funhouse, hotdogs, snow cones, the house of mirrors and a notoriously wild rollercoaster. We hoped to see our boyfriends there.

We screamed as we laughed on the rickety old rollercoaster. But it was all so soft, too, as if I was in an odd bubble, gently bumping into solid things, floating through that night. Sure, I was still me, but a new me, so full of joy, falling in love with everyone and everything in the whole world in a new way—more alive than I'd ever been.

It was a week or so later (at my Taco Bell night job) that the smell of the beans made me sick to my stomach, and a week after that when I missed my first period.

This year, with all of us quarantined in our own bubbles, we kept each other sane through COVID and chaos, still laughing at this rollercoaster life.

ADVICE FOR MY YOUNGER SELF...

If you have plans with your girlfriends, don't cancel for a guy.

Addendum to my advice…

My grandmother, born in 1888, had seven kids—five of them lived. As I write this, 131 years after her birthday, I try not to imagine how heartbreaking it must have been to lose her children. Grandma was so strong, and so gentle. She once rolled out of the car's front seat and into the road as my mom rounded a corner.

She then dusted herself off, said, Oh, my." and got back into our 1950 Chevy. To honor her, I reach into my memories and find the ten best from Grandma Munn:

Keep the floors clean.

Bathe the babies every night.

Keep the house warm.

Open the windows at night.

Save what may be useful.

Ask for help when you need it.

Use what you have.

Figure out how to make or fix things.

If you had it, find it.

If you can't find it, keep looking.

—Grandma Munn

Words To Live By

"Got my housework done, baked six loaves of bread, cooked a kettle of mush; put clothes away and set my house in order. At 9 pm, I was delivered of another son."

—1840 diary of Mary Walker, Oregon Museum

My Hero

Stephenie Natta

Teacher, college administrator and adventurer, born in Western Canada, Stephenie Natta enjoyed 33 years in New York studying, working, loving concerts and absorbing the culture. Excelling at fabric arts, her stories were, at one point, displayed in whimsical wall hangings and a line of flouncy lingerie. Classical music, and the prospect of a new project, continue to inspire her.

Live theatre and classical music have always added so much colour to my life; I've been an avid concert go-er and a subscriber and season ticket holder to theatre and music groups for many years.

And so it was, anticipating another entertaining play, dressed to the nines, I climbed the stairs to the theatre, opened the door and fell completely inelegantly in the lobby.

The world came running; the oldest man on the earth kindly extended his arms and said, "I'll help you." I immediately visualized both of us on the floor, immobile, so I declined his solicitous offer and suggestions from other people in the crowd.

After some time of pain and embarrassment, a faceless, melodious, masculine voice behind me said, "I'll help you."

I warily said, "I'm kind of heavy."

He replied, "I'm kind of strong."

With no time for further thought, he scooped me up from behind and set me on my feet. I was eventually able to turn, but never saw my benefactor because he disappeared quickly.

After the play, the Stage Manager sought me out and said, "Did you realize that your savior was one of the actors?"

There were only two men in the play; one was short and the other was of average height like me, so I knew which one had helped me.

From the playbook, I learned that the actor was from Edmonton. I wrote him a sincere letter of gratitude and sent it to the theatre to thank him. With tongue in cheek, I also asked him if he would say hello to my sister on his next Edmonton engagement. He never did. Sometimes one cannot depend on people.

MY FAVOURITE QUOTE...

"I didn't fall, I was testing gravity—it still works."

–Anonymous

ADVICE FOR MY YOUNGER SELF...

Keep a log or diary to record dates of career moves, health history, life-changing events and financial matters.

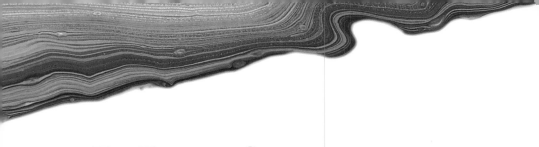

The Thrill of Sensation

Mandy Eve-Barnett

Mandy Eve-Barnett's passion for writing emerged later in life; she's making up for lost time. A multi-genre author, her work is based in love, nature, magic and mystery. With nine books published since 2011, more in the wings and freelance projects, Mandy regularly blogs and champions other writers. Secretary of her local writing group, while holding the position of past president of the Arts & Culture Council of Strathcona County, her creative life is lived to its fullest.

I have always enjoyed the thrill of physical sensations. It can be the oscillations of a swing, the twirl of a fairground ride, the acceleration of a vehicle, the rarified aspect of a great height or the gravity-defying takeoff of an aeroplane. I can sense the feeling of being swung around by my father or the bumpy rides in his wheelbarrow.

As a young woman, I enjoyed driving my car fast along English country lanes or riding pillion on a motorbike. The acceleration and the side to side to movement were such a buzz. One evening, I put on new wedge heels for a night out, mistakenly believing we were driving to the pub in a car. My ride arrived on a motorbike!

Too late to change, I donned a helmet, a warm jacket and settled on the seat. The pub was a favourite, several miles away along shaded, winding, high-hedged lanes. The motorcycle swung back and forth, dipping low around the sharp corners. A smile was fixed on my face as the summer wind blew onto my face, and the engine vibrated with acceleration and deceleration. My body was completely relaxed, swaying in perfect time with the action of the vehicle.

Finally, at our destination, I swung my leg over the motorcycle seat and promptly nearly fell. Puzzled, I looked at my feet to find the edge of my wedge shoes worn down on both outer edges. Ruined and not worth saving, I took them off. Luckily, it was a summer evening, and I could walk barefoot in the pub's garden. I wore them on the trip home, then discarded them. The lesson: make sure you wear proper footwear when riding a motorbike.

Advice To a Young Friend...

Don't forget to enjoy thrill-filled times that in life-affirming moments make your heart beat wildly...no matter how old you get. You are never too old to try something new. Pump your legs on that swing, or get someone to push you—higher, higher! Take time to embrace nature's glories, and let her gift you and fill you with experiences and sensations that throw you into a state of wonder.

CO-DEPENDENCY

Anonymous

Do you ever look back at your younger self and think about how far you've come? Bear in mind, by "younger self," that could mean last year or last week. I've looked back daily recently and with a proud smile, knowing that the person I am today is empowered by self-esteem.

I grew up in an emotionally traumatic household where, due to a combination of events including unstable personalities, lack of parenting skills to bring comfort and union, the bitter divorce of my parents and my social-services–assigned Big Sister repeatedly moving away without contacting me, I ultimately developed the belief that I wasn't loveable.

While I was fortunate to make friends with a number of wonderful people during my teen years, I would waffle between complete insecurity about our friendships, hurting friends in the process, or feel so frightened about trying to meet anyone new that I would hang on tightly and eventually lose the very friends who once cared so much for me.

This pattern continued for decades. My introvert personality made making friends difficult, and, not knowing what an introvert was, I constantly felt I was socially awkward and that there was something wrong with me. While I did succeed in finding a wonderful man, I will never forget our first date (which, by the way, was a blind date). While absolutely lovely and full of beautiful memories that we continue to celebrate to this day, I viewed the whole conversation, as well as all the conversations in dates after and up to our wedding, as tests.

Would this man love me? Never, in any of our dates, did it occur to me ever to think about whether he was the right person for me to spend my life with, or whether little things he would do that annoyed me were things I wanted to live with forever. I will say here, to answer this question, that, while there were many difficult years, yes, he was the right man! Thank goodness!!

During a difficult part of our marriage, and when I lost yet another friend to my need for constant contact and validation, I also came to learn about co-dependence. I joined a 12-step group, I read, I shared, I grew. As I worked through myself, I could feel self-esteem developing for the first time. Conversations with my husband became easier as I became better at communicating. I came to understand that being an introvert was something I cherished and fully accepted, rather than believing it was abnormal and awkward.

Along the way, I discovered Laughter Yoga, became a certified leader and developed self-confidence I had only felt in fleeting moments throughout my life. Now, I am so happy with who I have become and that all my relationships are healthy.

ADVICE FOR MY YOUNGER SELF...

It can take time to know yourself, to believe in yourself, to understand yourself. Take this time; it is so important for your mental health and healthy relationships. And, as you work through yourself, if you hit difficult times and wonder, *What's wrong with me?* know that you are always worth the time to figure out what it takes to feel the joy you deserve.

GIVE YOUR DREAMS A NAME

Susan Faye Young

Susan Young puts being a proud Mom and Nana first on her self-description list. After that, she describes herself as a payroll guru, having made an art out of her career of paying people. A lover of all kinds of music, especially jazz and southern rock, she loves to cook, entertain, travel, cycle and enjoys archery. She's always had a Boston terrier… or two…or three.

My two children, a daughter and a son, are adopted. For years I hoped for, longed for, wept for, a child that I did not have. I firmly believed—and still do—in the power of positive thinking and constantly visualized the little family that I wanted so badly.

Then a little blonde-headed two-year-old came into my life. On the day my husband and I met her, I was wearing sunglasses. She wanted a pair, so we took her to the store in search of child-sized ones. My husband went one way, she, in my arms, and I went another. Suddenly she was looking around as if lost. "What's the matter?" I asked.

"Momma, where is Daddy?" she replied.

At that moment, I knew I had found my daughter; she had called me my dream name—Momma.

One year later, I received a call from a doctor friend. He had delivered a baby boy and told me the baby's mother wanted him to help her find a home for the child; she wanted to meet us before she made her decision.

The meeting happened later that day. After a long conversation with her, she looked at me and asked, "What are you going to name him?" I spoke the name I had always wanted for my son.

She looked at me, smiled and said, "I like that name." In that moment she and I knew I had found my son. He had a name long before he was born; it was just waiting for him to arrive.

MY ONE PIECE OF ADVICE...

Clean up as you go.

This advice was given to me by my paternal grandmother when I was a young girl. I was always with her in the kitchen; her advice related to kitchen activities. I have found, however, that it is good advice for all situations in life. Clean up whatever you need to as you go, be it to apologize, to speak up about an injustice, to take the time to make a difference, to say thank you. You may not get another chance to clean up that particular issue or situation later.

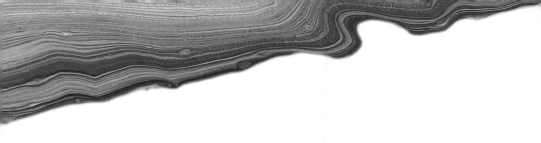

Fear Getting In the Way? Try Play

Erica Swiatek

Erica Swiatek's passion is play and creative thinking, which she weaves into her work in the field of learning and development.

In June 2020, amid the Covid-19 pandemic, I was teaching a class, virtually, for Buffalo State College called Creative Thinking & Problem Solving. The concept was reframing. Reframing is taking a statement like, "We don't have enough money" and changing it to a question or reforming it another way...something like, "How might we raise the funds?"

From time to time, while teaching the class, I experienced feeling blue. I had been laid off from my regular job; an extrovert, missing people, home alone a lot while my husband and children continued in jobs that required they attend in person. One particular blue day, I thought, *Hey, I teach reframing, so instead of thinking about the things Covid is taking away from me, why don't I think about the things Covid is giving me?*

Well, this led to the insight that what I had been given was time and freedom I might not have again for a while. My niece had just graduated from high school, so she and I went on an epic adventure, hopping in the car and driving to the Badlands. We slept under the stars, far away from people. I got to witness her experience buffalos and prairie dogs in the wild. We continued on to Yellowstone; again, we camped in the back country. This time, I got to see her see Old Faithful and the Grand Prismatic Springs. By this point we had only spent about $68 to camp. The next part of the trip was in the stunning setting of Bryce Canyon where we slept in a teepee; I took the opportunity to present a humor academy session from there. We ended our epic journey at the Grand Canyon...Kayla still talks about our adventures.

MY ONE PIECE OF ADVICE...

Never forget to reframe your thinking when you feel blue or stuck. Changing a statement to a question or flipping your thinking can open you to new possibilities.

MY FAVOURITE QUOTE...

"Play keeps us vital and alive. It gives us an enthusiasm for life that is irreplaceable. Without it, life just doesn't taste good."

–Lucia Capocchione

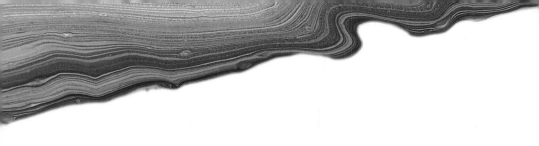

Do You Remember When? (DYRW)

Christina Silva

Christina Silva regards motherhood as the most important job she's ever had. Following that, of her many jobs and adventures, she ranks being a perinatal nurse and faculty member in joint second place. Now an adventurous empty nester, she's still deciding what she wants to be when she grows up and learning how to balance having a life with working to pay for her future exploits.

Those words always cause me to smile. One of my favorite Do You Remember When (DYRW) stories is a Thanksgiving afternoon around the dinner table with my three children. The youngest, Sarah, was sixteen or seventeen. She started with DYRW..."You never cooked from a box and always made everything from scratch?"

I chuckled and replied, "Do you remember why I never cooked from a box and always made everything from scratch?"

She replied with a no.

Again, I chuckled. "We were too poor to afford the box, but I could manage to buy the staples like flour, sugar, salt, eggs and just learned how to make everything from scratch. Now, I can afford the box and have no time to make everything from scratch."

This story makes me smile because, even though we were dirt poor, the kids did not know it. They knew that they had a house to live in, clothes to wear and good, homemade food to eat. They knew they were loved.

ADVICE FOR MY YOUNGER SELF...

Don't focus on how many material items you can give your kids and loved ones. Focus on how much you can love them. The love and time spent on them will outweigh the material things you could not afford.

WORDS TO LIVE BY

"The best gift you can give is a hug: one size fits all and no one ever minds if you return it."

–Marge Piercy, Writer and Activist

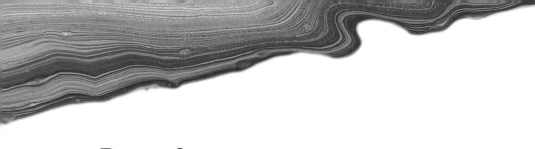

DIVING IN

Phyllis Dozier

Phyllis is a poet, screenwriter and memoirist. Finding her creative voice after thirty years as an HR executive at Fortune 100 companies, Phyllis Dozier takes writing classes at the Loft and is a member of Women of Words. A Phi Beta Kappa, B.A. summa cum laude and M.A. graduate of the University of Minnesota, she lives in Minneapolis and draws inspiration from nature's changing of the seasons.

To celebrate his seventy-fifth birthday, my father-in-law invited us to a weekend at Grandview Lodge, a resort in northern Minnesota that offered fishing, tennis, hiking and swimming. My husband, Chris, along with our two sons and I, were excited to enjoy a few hot July days at a posh resort.

Although our younger son, Cutler, knew how to dog paddle, he was eager to learn to dive. So, late on Saturday afternoon, I showed Cutler how to squat like a frog at the side of the pool, bend his head down, straighten his arms over his head and clasp his hands together. Then I gently tipped his butt up. As I did, he fell into the water and his legs straightened, a successful little dive.

He was thrilled. He practiced a few more before Chris appeared to tell us it was time to get ready for dinner.

But both boys wanted to keep swimming. Chris agreed to watch them while I showered, dressed, dried my hair and put on make-up. All put together, I returned to the pool to pick them up. Cutler was despondent. He was belly flopping and didn't know why. I watched him and, sure enough, he was looking up at the last minute, therefore slapping the water with his stomach.

I squatted down next to him, tucked my head and clasped my arms overhead.

Before I knew it, I fell into the pool. With all of my clothes on. When I came up for air, the boys were laughing, and Chris was holding out a towel, smiling. When we finally entered the restaurant, whose floor-to-ceiling picture windows overlooked the pool, the place erupted in applause. It took me a moment to realize I was the intended recipient. The diners had seen the whole thing. All I could do was take a bow.

ADVICE FOR MY KIDS AND FRIENDS...

"The only real failure is the failure to try, and the measure of success is how we cope with disappointment."

I love this quote from the *Best Exotic Marigold Hotel*. Whether it's falling into a swimming pool with all your clothes on, then taking a bow instead of walking out or it's kicking butt on your next assignment after hearing you didn't get the promotion, how we translate our failures into learning opportunities will ultimately determine how successful we are.

Divine Assistance
Albertine Coulombe

Raised in a French Catholic family of 16 children on a farm in central Alberta, Albertine Coulombe didn't speak English until age five. Farm life continued to play a role in her life after she started a family—two biological sons and a daughter, adopted when she was nine months old. Retired from thirty-five years teaching French kindergarten, the focus of her life consists of staying healthy, spending time with friends and family and participating in church events.

In the summer of 1966, my friend, Alice, and I were butchering chickens on our farm. It was an uneventful day until her two young boys ran toward us screaming that my two-and-a-half-year-old son, Dean, had fallen through an insecure trap door and plunged into the farm's well.

I ran to the well and found him face down, floating on top of the water. The shock of seeing him gave me the adrenalin to grab him, pull him onto the grass, and perform CPR, which I had never tried before.

As we didn't have a telephone, we ran to the car to transport him to the hospital located three miles away. To our dismay,

Alice had left the lights on in the car and, consequently, the battery was dead.

I heard the school bus in the distance and ran to the road informing the bus driver what had happened. His response was, "I can't do anything to help." My only option was to jump on my bike and peddle to the neighbour's a mile away. They drove me back to the farm and boosted the battery, allowing us to race to the hospital.

The doctor checked my son, giving us a good report, indicating the reason he had not drowned was because the water table was so high, and he was of light weight.

At that moment, as the news was delivered, I knew that there had to be a higher power; I could not have done what I did on my own power.

MY ONE PIECE OF ADVICE...

Enjoy single life until at least 30 years of age.

WORDS TO LIVE BY

"I do not know the word 'quit.'"

–Susan Butcher, first dog musher to win the Iditarod in Alaska in four out of five sequential years.

Say What!?

Rhonda Skinner

Rhonda Skinner worked for more than twenty years in a variety of human services jobs. At forty-five, she returned to university, earned a degree in Applied Communications and began a career as a writer and editor. In her spare time, she reads, plays golf, strums her ukulele and volunteers with WILDNorth, a wildlife rescue and rehabilitation centre.

When my doctor found a lump in my breast, she sent me for a mammogram and a biopsy. The tumor had to come out whether it was cancerous or not. That meant time off work, so I met with my supervisors, Dana and Grace, and told them I was waiting for biopsy results. They were both shocked and concerned that I might have breast cancer. Grace said, "Oh, Rhonda. When will you get your autopsy results?"

How does one respond to that question? Ignore the faux pas and let her save face? Gently correct her and lie about how others have made the same mistake? I got my answer when I looked at Dana. She was red-faced, had a hand over her mouth and was doubled over stifling laughter. That did it. We both cracked up. Grace went wide-eyed and slack-jawed when she realized what she'd said. That made us laugh even harder. I managed to squeak out, "That's a little premature, don't you think?" That set all three of us off. My cheeks and stomach were sore by the time we regained composure.

I'm happy to report that my cancer treatments were successful, and I've been healthy ever since. That exchange took place twenty-two years ago, and I still laugh about it today.

MY ONE PIECE OF ADVICE...

Unexpressed feelings eventually come out in unhealthy ways. Express your feelings. Laugh when you can, cry or vent when you need to. Be there for others, and allow others to be there for you.

ALL THOSE PRETTY LITTLE FISHES

Theresa Sarnecki

Lifetime volunteer Theresa Sarnecki secured a grant to attend university for one year and then became a teacher. Taking a break after each of her four children were born, she completed her second year of university through night and summer classes. An example of perseverance, it took twenty-five years to complete her education degree. Teaching in England cemented her love of travel. She and her husband traveled extensively, and after his passing, she continued. Most recently, at the age of eighty-six, she spent a wonderful month in India.

When my husband and I traveled to Australia with our friends, we had many funny experiences.

One that has always stayed in my mind is when my friend Sadie and I went off on our own. We had seen a posh resort from a distance and knew it had a private beach. We decided to walk through the lobby as if we belonged, then out the other side to the beach.

With hardly anyone in the water, we put on our snorkeling masks and headed into the pristine, blue-green sea. We weren't too far out when we found ourselves surrounded by stunning multi-colored fish. We were captivated, a fabulous experience.

All of a sudden, I became aware of splashing, screaming and floundering beside me. I righted myself in the shallow water then saw my friend sputtering, coughing and in a state of panic. A large school of small fish had swum in front of her (as they do with everyone) and she was sure they were going to go down the front of her bathing suit. She had panicked, and when she did, the snorkel came out of her mouth, she inhaled, then couldn't get her breath.

When I quit laughing (we weren't supposed to be there and didn't want to draw attention), I was able to calm her and convince her that the fish would swim around her. For the rest of the trip, we never let her forget that she nearly drowned because of those pretty little fishes.

WORDS TO LIVE BY

"Life is an adventure...dare it!"

–Mother Teresa, international missionary

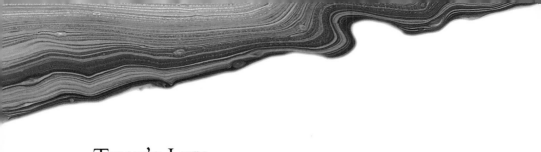

THAT'S LIFE
Loretta Schnepper

Married for 55 years, Loretta Schnepper had three children, worked as a medical technologist, had a small business and dabbled in floral arrangement. She enjoys gardening, exercising, baking, hiking, traveling and, more recently, talkback radio.

I met my husband shortly after he immigrated from Germany. He confided that he was lonely, hadn't made many friends and didn't know much about our Canadian way of life.

I invited him to a country dance, our first date.

One particular Saturday night, we went to a dance in the high school from which I had graduated. We met the principal, and he inquired what I was doing. I told him that I was at the university taking sciences. He then asked my husband (my boyfriend at that time) what he was doing. He proudly replied, "I'm going to university too, and I'm taking bricklaying."

My face turned red!

I didn't complete my science degree, but my husband completed his course at the technical school and became a top-notch bricklayer, working for 45 years in the trade.

For many of his later years, my husband suffered with dementia. As his memory and physical health deteriorated, he became dependent on my care. He was so grateful for everything I did for him. I'll never forget what he would tell anyone who came to visit, "My beautiful wife takes care of me, and I would be dead if it wasn't for her."

Those words tug at my heart strings and bring tears to my eyes every time I think of him.

MY ONE PIECE OF GOOD ADVICE...

Be honest and kind to all.

As you live your life, consider this quotation from Doris A. Wright: "The future lies before you, like a field of fallen snow; be careful how you tread it, for every step will show."

WORDS TO LIVE BY

"We need to be angels for each other, to give each other strength and consolation..."

–Henry Nouwen, Catholic priest, professor, writer and theologian

A KNOCK AT THE DOOR

Shelley Tincher Buonaiuto, *Wild Ride* sculptor

An artist whose family and friends are beloved to her, Shelley endeavors to be conscientious—and especially aware of her flawed, authentic self—and to see and speak truth through the lens of love she holds for others. Awestruck by nature, she embraces the knowledge of our oneness as we work to develop equitable social and economic structures. She wholeheartedly believes that the patriarchy, unable to transform itself, must be balanced by the empathy and relational awareness of women.

I was on the floor, working intently and with some anxiety, on a presentation about global warming I planned to deliver the next day to my climate change group. A certain frustration with the work was compounded by my serious concerns about my husband, every day losing more of his faculties to early onset dementia; it was essential to always know where he was and what he was doing. As I was trying to make the presentation clear by organizing my ideas, there came a knock on the front door. Somewhat annoyed by the interruption, I jumped up to open it. The other side of the threshold revealed two young women—one of them I perceived to be possibly of Mayan descent—each holding a bible. I waited for the standard line: Did I believe in the Good Book?

No, I didn't...Why were they doing this?

I paused to give them a little time to respond. Their youth and commitment was visible; there was something charming about them. Triggered in a stream of associations from long history of frustration with religion, I could barely control my eruption. My lecture went from the destruction by the ancient Hebrews of the matriarchal societies; the invention of a male god demanding obedience; the use of religion by power possessors to divide societies along authoritarian versus nurturant frames; scapegoating gays and women; 300 years of burning witches; the creation of money and how the economic system is designed to fatten the few and impoverish and enslave the rest. I offered examples of higher-thinking: quantum physics and zero point energy; a vast cosmic system beyond the physically perceivable; and of course, the brilliant contributions of the Mayans' advanced civilization to astronomy, while Europe thought the world was flat.

When they said they believed in Adam and Eve, I recounted my view of the real purpose of that myth, the demeaning of women by placing blame for all evil on a woman's sensuality. When I reached the part about the snake being a sacred symbol to the matriarchal societies, and so the creators of patriarchy had to turn it into a symbol of this "devil" guy, my husband, Michael, appeared at the door wearing no pants. "The devil," he said. "Now I can relate to that."

MY PIECE OF ADVICE...

I try not to give it, yet I know when I do it's always for myself, therefore, always listen carefully...to everyone, especially your Self.

Surrounded by Story Retreat
Breakout Room One

Come on in, there's a seat for you right here. Slip off your shoes; tuck your legs under if you like. This is the first breakout room in a writing sanctuary designed especially for you.

Picture yourself at a retreat in the setting of your choice. Feel at ease in your created setting—perhaps you have even curated a space within your own home. How wonderful: a chaise on your enclosed deck; a hammock in a peaceful, warm setting; your favourite armchair in a book-lined office; your sofa, complete with a favourite blanket, in front of the fireplace; a little tent, complete with pillows and comfort items, that you've set up in the basement. Make sure your tea or water is handy, so you are ready to make this experience your own.

As you have experienced in the Storytellers' recollections, every aspect of our lives can be a story. The negative ones pop up in our mind quickly. The lessons they teach us can help keep us safe. Often they are driven by strong emotion and, as we recall them, the details can be vibrant.

It's easy to recall the hotel fire in Mexico City and the scary details of running down a smoke-filled corridor and sitting outside on the pavement wrapped in a blanket. The rest of the trip, however, fades into, "I guess it was a good time…nothing bad happened." As mentioned before, it's important to remember that often the positive aspects of an experience are folded into the ordinary, and on recall, the details can be hidden from us.

This retreat focuses on nurturing our positive memories, the ones that we want to enjoy in the years to come. Positive memories bring positive emotions, and these make our lives happier and more satisfied.

In the journaling pages, you will encounter stories and diverse topics to tickle your curious mind. Among all your notes, do some of your own memories emerge as ones that delight you, that you want to keep fresh for recall in the future?

**The more we recall positive memories
the stronger they become.**

All the Storytellers shared events from their lives in their own authentic voice; there was no filtering for age, topic or writing experience.

As you read the stories, did any of the images of the Storytellers remind you of anyone?

In the stories, did you feel drawn to doodle in the wide margins? I hope so.

Make notes here, too. Or shapes. Or pictures.

Imagine the opening stories were presentations from which you walk away with a nugget that resonated with you…a word, a phrase, an image. Let that be the catalyst for your own creation. Return and ask one or two or five of the women to tell their story again. Sit right beside them, a solo audience and allow yourself to absorb their message.

Freely use the resources offered in all areas. Be you. And, if you have forgotten, then find yourself between the lines. There will be stories that resonate with you, prompts that will compel you to respond, some will do the opposite. Of the latter, sit with them a little; some of the best ideas come from being courageous enough not to turn away from a subject.

Spread your reflections and ideas across a fresh page.

THE TEN TOPIC WRITING STRATEGY

Some years ago, I went to a writers' conference to attempt to figure out "the how-to" of writing. The leader, a prolific, published author, gave us all a starting point. She suggested we each identify ten topics from our life before our twelfth birthday, then write a few paragraphs on each. Her examples included memories, such as a best friend at school, religion in family, earliest memory, Grandma's kitchen, places lived and a favourite pet.

When I followed her advice, vivid details and powerful emotions flowed through me; I had not realized events—positive and negative—had been so profoundly encoded to memory.

> I was eleven years old and miserable; my sister had a beautiful, new dress because she was graduating from high school. I had just argued with my mother about my having to do more chores. I ran up to my bedroom (shared with that same sister), grabbed one of her new high heels, and threw it at the wall. The heel pierced the gyprock, pinning the shoe to the painted wall. It remained impaled. In shock over what I'd done and the results, I panicked, anticipating the worst reaction of my family. But as I looked at it from all angles, the shoe in the wall looked so funny. I started giggling, and, being a problem solver, began looking for bubblegum to plug the hole.

Although this memory reflects a difficult situation, my natural inclination for silliness and a sense of the ridiculous diffuses the negativity. Changing the perspective and focusing on the humour of the situation modifies the tone of the story. The memory continues to bring me a sense of satisfaction.

Reframing is a great strategy. In Erica Swiatek's *Wild Ride* story, she refers to the benefits of reframing.

If you were to employ this writing strategy, which ten general topics would you choose from your early years?

1.

2.

3.

4.

5.

6.

7.

8.

9.

10.

ENDLESS STORIES

"Stories never really end…even if the books like to pretend they do. Stories always go on. They don't end on the last page, any more than they begin on the first page."

–Cornelia Funke, *Inkspell*

If there is a Storyteller in this section whose story has touched you, who is it and why?

If any of the situations reminds you of an experience in your family's life, which are they? Share the connection.

Is there a word of advice that speaks to your heart?

What advice could you offer your younger self?

Memoir or Not?

As you review your memories, is there an event you wish you had documented? Can you share some details about it?

Are there stories swirling around you now? Can you outline them here for later?

Are you drawn to writing about real life experiences, as in a memoir, or do you see yourself as a fiction writer? What genre? Is there a poet inside you? Explore the *whys* of your choices.

Further information about writing memoirs:
National Association of Memoir Writers, www.namw.org

It's Your Turn To Be a Co-author

When I've approached women to submit a story for this project, I often heard, "I don't have a story."

In digging a little deeper, it became clear that many women felt they would like to offer a funny or positive story, and yet it was difficult to come up with one. That seems to go along with some of the research that suggests that negative events are remembered more easily than the positive. Sometimes a positive story is sitting there waiting for you. Other times, you have to dig a little deeper around what seemed like a partially negative experience.

If you have your own funny or positive story that you could have added to this *Wild Ride* collection, what would it be called? What might be an overview?

What's the funniest thing that ever happened to you or your family?

How are you doing? Do you need a break? Another cuppa?

This is your safe haven, so take care of you...body and soul.

Be gentle with yourself.

> "Self-care is giving the world the best of you,
> instead of what's left of you."
>
> –Katie Reed

IMAGINATION STATION

Imagine a warm, sunny day. You are strolling along a familiar country lane. Your gaze is unfocused, but you recognize that perfect climbing tree, a broken fence surrounding a farmed field and an old building in the distance.

What can you smell, hear, taste? What will you touch? How will that feel? If the scene was a postcard, how would you describe it?

Where does this imagery take you? A memory? A wish?

GRATITUDE STRATEGY

There are many ways to establish a gratitude practice. Letter writing, not as a thank you for a gift, but to express appreciation to someone who has impacted your life, can be cathartic and transformational. Perhaps it's your mom, a favourite teacher, a friend from the past, a current cohort, a coach or a supervisor. Describe in detail what he or she did for you and exactly how it affected your life; mention how you often remember his or her efforts. Positive energy will be generated regardless of whether or not you send the letter.

For example: "I will never forget our conversations; you went out of your way to treat me like an adult…pretty heady stuff for a seventeen-year-old kid."

List three people and make some notes about the details of your appreciation.

WHAT A CHARACTER!

Some people are so singularly on their own path that they are unforgettable. In my journey, the combination of an outlandish costume and burned popcorn make for a perfect memory.

In the initial stages of our toy adventure, we entered our first U.S. trade show by subletting a table from Bud, who had a booth and too little product. Our booth-mate was a good looking, seventy-year-old garrulous exhibitor with a full head of curly grey hair, handsome in his own way and obviously well known and loved on the exhibition floor. We learned that he was a seasoned exhibitor who traveled from show to show, living in an RV that was parked outside the convention hall.

Bud's exhibitor wardrobe was a showstopper—a bright yellow shirt coupled with cotton tropical lime green trousers that were splattered with massive pink hibiscus flowers. At one point during the trade show, Bud pulled out his electric corn popper and became the entertainer to his fellow exhibitors. Within moments, smoke billowed from the back of the booth. The corn popper caught fire and security closed down the fun. The memory of the experience with Bud always makes me smile. What a character!

Who are the unforgettable characters (fictional and/or real) that have passed through your life?

You are an unforgettable character too—quirky or otherwise. To whom are you unforgettable? Why?

JUST ONE, PLEASE

Describe your best day in the future. Where will you be? Who else is there? Immersed in the memory, what can you taste, smell, feel, hear, see? Why is it memorable?

Do You Remember When (DYRM)?

Author and story contributor Christina Silva shared a heartfelt family story called "Do You Remember When?"

Kitchen-table stories often share our deepest values and beliefs. Can you recall a DYRW story in your life? What is it you remember? Who are the people sitting with you?

I Am Somebody

Writing, or any creative endeavor, (cooking, gardening, writing, magic) takes time, attention and commitment.

"Whatever you can do or dream you can, begin it; boldness has genius, power and magic in it."

–Credit to poet, John Anster (Ireland) as paraphrasing when translating the work (Faust) by Johann Wolfgang von Goethe (Germany).

Write about a project you once invested yourself in, or an effort from the past in which you were fully dedicated. Be sure to include all your senses when you share.

When you are finished, comment on whether it has evoked specific wants and needs. Is there something new that is calling to you? What is it?

A ROOM WITH YOUR VIEW

Use this space to express your own memories, hopes, dreams and feelings in words, jottings, pictures or doodles.

A ROOM WITH YOUR VIEW

2

MEMORIES AND EMOTION

Keynote: Memories and Emotion

Highlights

- The stronger the emotion the more vivid the memory

- Negative memories are often remembered more vividly than positive ones

- Memories are not indelible—positive and negative memories fade over time

- On recall, we can colour memories as better or worse

- Gratitude can improve retrieval of positive memories

- Use positive memories to increase positive emotions

- Use mental imagery to actively savor recalled positive memories

The connection illustrated in family stories is a generational gift… priceless.

Before I started school, I was the little kid playing under the kitchen table and paying attention to the stories that my father was sharing. They were tales of hardship, of his father coming to this country, building a sod house for the family, clearing the land and playing the violin to make extra money for the family.

More recently, I had the privilege of spending a weekend each month with my mother in the final years of her life. At 93 years of age, her memory was excellent despite her failing health. During that time, she loved to tell me stories of her early life. After she passed, I realized there were stories that she came back to time and again. It seemed as if her memories and those of my father, had been strengthened by events of strong emotion: fear, drama, disillusionment.

These experiences with my parents caused me to wonder what kind of memories I will return to in my later years. I grew up in a normal, small town environment, so I had been part of some good times. In their later years, I wondered why their dominant memories were so dark. What role does emotion have in retaining memories? What can I do now to improve the recall of stories that warm my heart and bring satisfaction?

Just as we use a highlighter to bring our attention to text, emotion strengthens memories.

Those of us around in the sixties know where we were when John Kennedy was assassinated or what we were doing on 9/11. Negative information is often recalled with a greater sense of vividness and visual detail than the positive.

Although it is wonderful to remember the good times, these events, fantastic as they were, tend to fold themselves into the ordinary, and we may later reminisce over that night as a lovely experience, but not necessarily recollect the details with clarity.

This memory from my early life is detailed, clear and accessible.

Our family routinely attended church every Sunday. My Father, a Polish immigrant, insisted that, once a year, we attend a service in his language, even though it was unfamiliar to the rest of us, rarely spoken at home. As well, the one church with a Polish service was far away and in a district we rarely traveled. So, annually, we made our pilgrimage to a small country church that held only twelve pews. At that time, our family consisted of my parents, three school-aged children and one-year-old baby, Patricia.

When we entered, we saw that the church was overflowing. All eyes were on us as we paraded to the one empty front pew. While we waited for the service to begin, even the baby seemed to be feeling the embarrassment of the moment and sat quietly beside our mother. As the service started, we all stood and, at that moment, baby Patricia gave a piercing screech and continued screaming, obviously in great pain. In a span of time that seemed endless, we discovered a crack in the pew. When we all stood up at once, the back of baby's thigh had been pinched in the crack. Baby Patricia could not be calmed. The service was halted. Our family fled the church, ran to our car and drove home.

I don't recall my father ever mentioning the need to make that trip again.

When I recall this, I re-live every emotion, as if I were nine years old and in the church again—bored, feeling awkward, embarrassed, shocked at baby's screech, regretful for her great pain and relief that we wouldn't have to go there again. The details, including my favourite blue hat with the grosgrain ribbon, flow with great clarity.

Studies show that with the passing of time, our memories—while vivid in detail—are not indelible; they may not be totally accurate. Based on our mood at the time of recollection, we can colour the memory as significantly worse or better than the actual event.

Given the insight that negative events easily spring to mind in vivid detail, I better understand the reason for negative memories to repeat themselves in my parents' recollections.

In regard to sustaining positive memories, supported by research, it is reassuring to discover that that we can train our brain to think in ways that enhance positive memories. Taking time to think about the things in life for which we can be grateful can improve the retrieval of positive memories and promote mental well-being.

Further, we can use a well-studied technique to actively recall happy times and, through mental imagery and sensory exploration, make the positive memory more long-lasting. The more we recall positive memories, the stronger they become.

FLASHED IN FALLUJAH

Kelly Hayes-Raitt

Kelly Hayes-Raitt was press
credentialed by the Jordanian
government as she entered Iraq in
July 2003, three months after the
U.S.-led invasion. She reported live
from Baghdad, Fallujah, Hilla and
Basra via satellite phone to various
American news outlets. One of her
columns in the Santa Monica *Daily
Press* led to a Congressional
investigation into U.S.
subcontracting practices. "Flashed in
Fallujah" originally appeared in
Travelers' Tales *Leave the Lipstick,
Take the Iguana.* She now coaches
authors and edits books and blogs
at JumpStartMyBook.org.

While it is still just another angry Iraqi city, months before it will
become a major flashpoint in U.S./Iraqi relations, I tour Fallujah.

I am investigating war damage at a water treatment plant, several
weeks after President Bush's declaration of mission accomplished,
when a man exposes himself to me. He had been brushing close
against me as I walked along the narrow sidewalks that separated
the water treatment ponds, the folds of his shoulder-to-ankle robe
commingling uncomfortably with my long skirt in the 115-degree

heat. I'd pulled my purse in front of me, defensively elbowing space between us.

It is during my interview with the water district manager about her staff's heroic efforts to keep the water flowing through the first onslaught of war, when this strange man squats unobtrusively in a doorway, catches my eye and lifts his dishdasha, displaying how Allah had been very, uh, generous to him.

I'm shocked! *And* awed.

Talk about weapons of mass distraction! What's a white girl in a war zone to do? Being flashed in Fallujah isn't covered in a handbook for human rights.

I feel cornered. Should I speak up and risk offending my hosts? Or should I pretend nothing is happening? Even though he's the one who'd been naked, I'm the one feeling exposed. As a woman, as a westerner and especially as an American, I am vulnerable in this town that is already pretty edgy. Later this afternoon, I will be warned that certain powers in Fallujah vow to "kill an American a day" in retaliation for U.S. troops' gunfire exchange with locals who had taken refuge in a school. Schools are revered in Iraq, and the USA's blanketing one with bullets had further ignited this rebellious community.

But bullies bank on our staying politely silent. Whether deceptive governments or creepy deviants, these bullies profit when we react more to our own reactions than to the underlying aggression.

"That man exposed himself to me!" I point at him as stiffly as he had to me.

My male translator looks at me, confused. This gentle man, whose religious practice keeps him from even shaking hands with the opposite gender, repeats something in Arabic to the water treatment workers gathered around us. Meanwhile, in the confusion, the exhibitionist skulks out.

My outburst causes quite the stir! Workers run after the man, mortified that his aberrant behavior might reflect on them. Others make such a fuss with their apologies. I begin to feel guilty.

"It was no big deal." I offer, rolling my eyes. "Really, *it* was no *big* deal," I lie.

Apparently, one of the men understands my double-entendre, because he bursts out laughing, easing the tension.

We lose so much in war, and humour is right there with truth among the first casualties. Standing in battle-scarred Fallujah, a stranger and I start the rebuilding by bonding over a worn pun, proving that when we're brave enough to speak the truth, what really gets exposed is our humanity.

MY FAVOURITE QUOTE...

People may forget what you said, but they never forget how you made them feel.

–a well-loved sentiment shared by
Carl W. Buehner, Maya Angelou, and others.

My Adventurous Heart

Josephine Baranieski

Married for 69 years, Josie Baranieski enjoys family life and spending time with her loving husband. She cherishes her five children, thirteen grandchildren and eleven great-grandchildren.

I was born in November 1928, the eldest of three daughters. My father came to Canada at the age of seven, my mother when she was twenty-one. My father and his two brothers moved to individual farm sites in the same district in Saskatchewan. Although they lived close to each other by today's standards, back then, moving with wagons and horses was a long process.

Times were difficult, and all family members helped each other as much as possible. As the eldest son, my father held many responsibilities. My role in the family was to provide help to my mother and father, which included many outdoor activities: general farm chores, milking, tending to the animals, assisting at harvest and stooking sheaves. And there was school to attend, plus the required time to get there and back.

There was very little time to play as children are able to now.

During my adventures to get the cattle for milking or tending to them as they grazed, I came to spend time with many animals and birds in the wild. One particular summer, when I was about ten, I noticed an owl nesting in a tree. Being curious, I waited for the mother owl to leave the nest, then I climbed the tree. There were eggs that she had been sitting on. Each day I checked her nest; then one day there were hatchlings—baby owls. As the chicks got more feathers they became balls of fluff...oh, so cute. I became brave and took them out of their nest to watch them, but mother owl was not pleased, and I stopped my visits.

My walks were enjoyable and educational—watching ducklings, checking out rabbits—those moments left me respecting nature and taking in each day as a new adventure.

As I got older, married and had children, I still had the desire to enjoy the outdoors. I grew a large garden and spent many hours tending it. I exposed my children to all kinds of creatures and taught them how to look after their pets. I would take my children for little hikes so they could learn to enjoy the beauty of nature. We took mini-vacations to the nearby lakes and a trip to the Rocky Mountains where we enjoyed little day hikes.

As time went on, my husband and I would go camping and travelled many places within our country and abroad. We saw places that, as a child, I could never imagine I'd get to see. At times I had to persuade my husband to try new places—and I was successful, he did! My curious and adventurous personality had me wanting to see and experience how other people lived and what their surroundings were about.

Today we are unable to take long journeys because of our age, mobility and some health issues. Several years ago, we made the move from our rural farm home to a seniors' complex in a small city. Another adventure.

MY ADVICE TO OTHERS...

Go explore the world! Seek your adventures. Do not hesitate if you have the desire. There is so much to see and appreciate in our world. Nature warms the soul and, when you return home, you feel blessed to know what you have.

WORDS TO LIVE BY

"If we were meant to stay in one place, we would have roots instead of feet."

–Rachel Wolchin, author

Family Baseball Game
Carla Howatt

A communications professional, author, former politician, wife and mother, Carla Howatt is passionate about helping people, bringing awareness to mental health issues and disability challenges, and sharing stories.

I can still picture it: both sides of my extended family, spread out across the baseball field, moving slowly after a heavy thanksgiving meal. There is much goofing around and joking.

Adam comes up to the plate. At four years old, he is of small stature. With some effort, and almost more coordination than he had, he lifts the bat and rests it on his shoulder. Grampa, the pitcher, moves in closer, and Adam's youngest uncle comes over and puts his arms around him, hand-over-hand, to help him swing.

Grampa's pitch comes slow and high. Adam and his uncle swing and make contact with the ball. The crowd goes wild. Running almost faster than his little legs can carry him, he follows his dad's shouted directions. As he hits first base, Grampa, the pitcher, fumbles the ball for the second time, and it rolls between his legs and toward Adam's uncle who is on second base. As luck would have it, the second baseman isn't able to catch the ball and accidentally kicks it out into the field.

Adam's dad cheers him on and encourages him to go to second base. He makes it with ease as the outfield seems to be having problems finding the ball. Puffing now, he runs to third base.

The crowd goes crazy! They begin to shout directions to the little boy.

"Go Home! Run home!"

"Get a homerun! Run Adam, run home!"

Not wanting to disappoint his fans, Adam turns on his heels and runs as fast as he can…toward "home." We are confused and call him back. He is as confused as we are. Everyone has told him to "run home," and that is what he is doing, pointed toward "home," two blocks away.

MY ONE PIECE OF ADVICE...

If I could offer one piece of advice to my younger self, it would be to slow down, to stop wishing the years away and enjoy the moment. To hug Adam more, yell less and eat more chocolate.

SMALL SPACES
Jana Grzenda

Jana Grzenda is a former newspaper columnist. She has also published under the name Jana Barracks. She lives in Longmont, Colorado, with her family.

I bought my first condo in Boulder, Colorado, shortly after I turned twenty-seven. It was so small (about 400 square feet) that everything I owned had either two purposes or fit inside of something else. My coffee table was a trunk that stored winter sweaters. The loveseat opened into a hide-a-bed. My dining table could be rolled into a corner for just me or pulled out to seat a crowd of four.

One morning, I was getting ready for work and plowing through the closet of my tiny bedroom, looking for something cute and clean for the office. Nothing worked. Frustrated at the pile of rejects on my bed, I turned to making breakfast. With no toaster,

I placed my whole wheat bread under the oven broiler and returned to my closet. A few minutes later, the smoke detector raised the alarm, and I knew my toast was, well, toast.

I dashed to the kitchen, looking for a chair to stand on so I could disengage the alarm. My only other living room furniture was a rocker, and my dining chairs were on wheels. I pulled the rocker over and carefully climbed on it, hoping it wouldn't send me flying as I swung at the alarm.

That's when I realized my blinds were open. And I was naked.

LESSON LEARNED...

A toaster is not too big for a small apartment.

WORDS TO LIVE BY

"Friends are like clothes in the closet. Some are as comfortable as blue jeans. Others wear like pink turkey feathers."

–Jana Grzenda

A Moving Experience
Alicia Robinson

Alicia Robinson loves to write, mostly humorous pieces. Her maiden name is Canal, and her nickname from college is Panama. One of her favourite sayings is: "Laughter is God's hand on the shoulder of a troubled world." Married twenty-nine years to an awesome man, they live on the Eastern Shore of Maryland with their two wonderful dogs.

The screeching created by our van yanking the awning away from the building was hideous, an assault to the ears. Our van? No, "the van." A 24-foot moving van, rented to us by the company that had lost the key to the 8-foot moving truck we had reserved. The building? A small dry-cleaning business in Salt Lake City, Utah, with a drive-through lane and pick-up window, both covered by an awning (before we arrived). The reason we were at the dry cleaners? We weren't really. We were using its through road. I had told my husband I didn't think we could make it through the drive-through, but it was the only place to pull away from the store where I bought a diet soda to relieve stress, fatigue and frustration. At least I didn't say, "I told you so."

We were moving across the country to Maryland, where my husband had a new job as a professor. We had to get there for his orientation and had planned a reasonable traveling pace, seven-ish to eight-ish hours each day.

Our mandated stop at the dry cleaners changed that. First my husband had to call the owner of the business and promise our firstborn. Then he called the insurance company, which advised us that we had met our large deductible, in a small trip, less than a mile from our former residence.

Next, we awaited a representative from the truck company, who determined that the van wasn't safe to drive because of the seven-by-two-and-a-half-foot gap in its side. I again resisted the urge to utter, "I told you so."

We couldn't get another vehicle that day. We weren't sure where to take the behemoth van that, by the way, was towing our car. Our friends had small houses and lived in neighborhoods that barely accommodated compacts. The closest family member was in a different time zone. We couldn't even get into our old apartment anymore.

We found a truckers' hotel. My husband spent the next two days calling the headquarters of the vehicle rental company. He was put on hold at least thirteen times and repeated our saga at least seventeen-and-a-half times. On his last call, he let loose with every known swear word (and some unknown ones). We didn't know that on the other end of the line was a sweet, old man. He gently guaranteed us a normal-sized truck in exchange for the giant van.

Soon (with added insurance) we were rushing across the country—to the extent that you can rush with a moving truck towing a car, since they begin violently trembling over fifty-five miles an hour. This is why you never see one pulled over.

We straggled through the door of our apartment in Maryland a little after midnight, eight hours before the orientation, which he got to on time. He came back later that day, telling me, "They said I could have skipped today, and maybe part of tomorrow."

I wished I could have said, "I told you so," but I couldn't. I needed another diet soda.

MY ONE PIECE OF ADVICE...

Try never to say, "I told you so," unless it is a positive affirmation.

WORDS TO LIVE BY

"We cannot solve a crisis without treating it as a crisis. And if solutions within the system are so impossible to find, then maybe we should change the system itself?"

–Greta Thunberg, climate change activist and
2019 Person of the Year

My Mother, the Shopper

Nancy Franklin

Retired and working on her second chapter—writing about life and its absurdities, wherever and whenever she finds them—Nancy Franklin's work can be found at mirthquakes.com

My mother was an astute shopper. In foreign cities, she would wander down the aisles of markets, her keen eye discerning the authentic from the manufactured. She was naturally curious about and interested in everything, endearing herself to the locals with endless questions about their crafts. As a result, she was often taken down back alleys and cobblestone streets to the unmarked, dimly lit shops of artists who had created spectacular pieces.

She bargained hard and relentlessly. My father used to tell stories of our mother returning day after day to the shops of merchants, wearing them down with her charm. Eventually, the merchants succumbed to her obvious love of their pieces. Which explains how my parents' home ended up a showcase for masks; a carved Thai spirit house; Marionettes from Paris; pipes from an English church organ; a coffee table with legs from an old Indian charpai; and an ostrich-sized, brightly colored, papier-mâché bird.

This latter piece—the bird—was obtained on a trip my husband and I took with my mother to an art festival in Mexico. She had just been diagnosed with cancer, a type for which no treatment is effective. Her doctor told her to go; drink as many margaritas as she wanted.

My husband and I love to travel. But he's a museum-church-battleground monument kind of guy. He hates shopping. Which was why my mother and I, on that Mexican trip, were both stunned to hear my husband say, "Wow, look at this!" while wandering through yet another shop.

We both expected "this" to be something in dark wood—a bar maybe—or a deer head, something with a heavy, masculine feel. But he had affixed his gaze, and new-found art appreciation, on a four-foot-tall clay Catrina, brightly colored, with the skeletal head wearing a scarf and a massive hat, both covered in painted monarch butterflies. The figure nipped in dangerously at the waist, while the skirt, which formed the base, ballooned out in butterfly cut outs.

"This reminds me of the monarch butterflies in our backyard," he said, then turned to the merchant. "How much is this?" My mother and I sat down to watch the ensuing show.

She'd said she'd never seen him buy anything before; she was completely amused and enthralled by the negotiations and arrangements for shipping. For the rest of the trip, she couldn't stop talking about the Catrina statue.

A couple of weeks after we got home, the statue arrived, shattered. My husband was devastated, as was my mother. I told my husband to keep the pieces, and I would see what I could do with them.

Mom passed a few weeks later. Several museums expressed interest in some of the pieces she had collected—many pieces are now displayed in those places: Seattle; Galena, Illinois; South Dakota; and a hospital in Alaska. I know she would be pleased.

As for the Catrina? It took me three months to put her back together. The work was painstaking, but, as my husband says, it was a labor of love and remembrance. To both him and my mother.

MY ONE PIECE OF ADVICE...

Go fearlessly. Which is not the same as saying "be fearless." No one can truly be fearless. But to conquer fear and go fearlessly, means taking the chance on a life well-lived, with no "what-ifs."

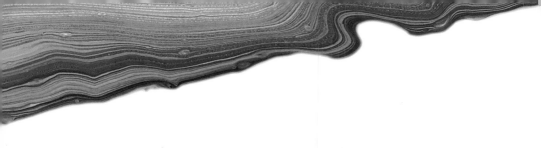

WHAT'S THE CHEAPEST HOUSE YOU'VE GOT?

Jacqueline Jeynes

Living in Wales, UK, Jacqueline Jeynes has been married for forty years to her second husband with whom she has a blended family of eight children, twenty grand-children and seven great-grandchildren. Returning to university later in life, she obtained a BEd (Hons) teaching degree, started her own training company, went on to receive an MBA and later a PhD. Jacqueline has been a nonfiction writer since 2000s.

In 1976, the hottest summer for decades, and after ten years in an abusive marriage, I had finally escaped. At twenty-eight, with five sons between two and nine, each of us with a carrier-bag of belongings, we fled to social housing miles away. Even though it was a new housing estate, the agency assumed because I had five children and no husband, we must be as rough as anything so they put us in the worst area. My children were frightened to leave the house.

With no maintenance (alimony) ever received, I had to return to work. Fortunately, I secured a good job at Inland Revenue (IRS).

I soon realised we had to leave the house. The first thing I did was check how much mortgage I could qualify for on my salary: £7000 (remember this is 1977). I filed this away.

On one of my days off, I visited nearby Worcester for some shopping. Opposite the train station, all the estate agents' (realtors) offices were in a line. On a whim, I went in.

"What is the cheapest house you've got?" I took a young man by surprise.

Flustered, he shuffled a few papers and told me £11,000.

My reply came swiftly: "No, sorry. Too expensive."

On I went to the next one.

"What is the cheapest house you've got, please?"

The young lady looked through the files. "Hmm, I think around £10,000 is the cheapest."

"What about that one—is it £8,500?" I pointed to a leaflet on the desk.

"Oh, yes, it has just come in. It's a big old house but was made into two separate rented homes. The owner had nothing but trouble with tenants so just wants to sell it." She smiled. "It is a bit of a state, but would you like to view it?"

It sounded perfect to me. "Will she accept £8,000? I am a first-time buyer, and a mortgage amount has already been agreed."

"Well, I can ask. Do you want the keys to view it? It isn't far."

"No, I don't care where it is or what it looks like." Now I was smiling. "Please check if £8,000 is acceptable."

Clearly bemused, she phoned, explained, and the seller accepted the offer.

"Brilliant! I will take it. I'll go and sort out the details now."
I provided my contact information."

"Erm... do you want to see it maybe?"

"Okay, I'll go and look, but this is a definite offer. Thanks for your help."

I admit, the next bit was probably not strictly legal. At the loan company down the street, I asked for a £1,000 loan to "redecorate," based on my salary. This was the deposit.

The beautiful, old house, with a hole in the wall where a door should have been, four big bedrooms and two bathrooms, was perfect. I sold it for £16,000 one year later, paid off the mortgage and loan, and bought a house around the corner for £11,500. A bargain!

A BIT OF ADVICE...

Take risks but be a calculated risk-taker.

Always make plans on the basis that half of those plans won't happen...but, if you don't plan anything, nothing will happen.

Make sure you understand how money works.

A Story of Jubilation After Conquering Fear

Cecilia Dunn

Recently retired, Cecilia enjoys her family and adventures in travel. Growing up in rural Saskatchewan, she attended technical school and worked in business. She stayed home with her two children until they began school then returned to work. Continuing education has always been an important part of her life.

My story begins on a small farm in Saskatchewan. The eldest of five children, I started school at the age of six. There was no kindergarten, so it was straight into a classroom with four grades and one teacher. Those were such scary and intimidating times for me. I was afraid of the older students, and as a result, I didn't want to put up my hand in class when the teacher asked questions for the fear of being laughed at, just in case my answer was incorrect.

Our farm home was close to the village; we could see the grain elevators there. On nice winter evenings, we would walk into our village and go ice-skating on an outdoor rink. I always convinced my younger sister to go into the warm-up shack ahead of me to see who was all there before I would go in to put on my skates. Once again, fearful someone might make fun of me or ask me a question. On those evenings, after skating, we would walk to the local café to wait for one of our parents to pick us up, and, one more time, my sister or younger brothers were sent ahead to see who was in the café, so I could decide if I would enter or wait outdoors for our ride home.

Eventually, I became more comfortable with who I was. At age twelve I joined our local 4-H Homecraft Club, and that started to provide me with more interaction.

Midway through grade ten, we discovered our high school was closing for the next school term. Most of the students were going to get bussed to the neighbouring town that had classrooms for every grade, a gymnasium and classes for typing and home economics. Most of us were excited, but once again, that fear was starting to build.

The first day at the new high school went well. I had some schoolmates with me, and I got to meet a few more people that I could call friends. I started to feel comfortable in my surroundings. It was exciting to go and watch school sports in the gym; I was exposed to school clubs like the school newspaper club, drama club and house leagues. Then it was announced that we were going to have the annual school dance held at the local community hall. How exciting was that?

Finally, the night of the dance arrived. I had a new outfit, my hair done fancy and makeup perfectly applied—complete with false eyelashes. One of my new girlfriends had purchased false lashes for herself and an extra set for me. We got ready at her house… it was so exciting.

The evening began, lights were dimmed on the full dance floor. A fellow student asked me to slow waltz. My head rested on his shoulder for several dreamy, slow dances, then the music stopped and everyone on the dance floor gathered in small groups to chat. All of a sudden, one of the other fellows in our small group says to my dance partner, "Bob, what's that behind your ear?" Bob reached behind his ear and lifted one of my false eyelashes that had latched onto him. I stood facing everyone with only one eyelash on. Well, the laughter started, and I was one of the laughers engaged in a deep belly laugh. The whole scene was hilarious.

But it was more than that…

At that moment, I realized I could laugh with others, even when the laugh was on me. No one was judging me. It just was simply a hilarious scene. My little mishap hit the school newspaper; it remains one of my fondest memories.

As years went by, I found my voice to educate and express myself; I continued growing with confidence. One of my greatest moments in self-improvement was to attend a Dale Carnegie course which was life changing and helped my career.

MY ONE PIECE OF ADVICE...

I would encourage anyone who has a fear of speaking out and communicating verbally to find an event that is humorous so that you can share stories and laughter with others. Humour opens many doors for friendship and inner growth.

I Once Bought a House with Three Credit Cards

Jacqueline Jeynes

In the late 1980s, the UK government decided to sell off some of the council-owned, social housing stock to sitting tenants. Unfortunately, much of it was concrete, built during the 1950s, so it was not considered mortgageable unless upgraded with brick outer walls.

I have five sons. Number three son had been working in Saudi Arabia, leaving behind my wonderful daughter-in-law, Margy, and their two beautiful children, my precious grandsons. Sadly, it came to be known he was not coming home.

As Margy had been renting the house for more than ten years, she became eligible—as part of a government scheme—to buy it at a vastly reduced price; a wonderful opportunity to own instead of rent. But there were several problems to overcome.

Although her salary was enough to cover a mortgage, she had no funds for a deposit. A mortgage, even with a deposit, wasn't possible because of the concrete structure rules. She'd need a loan. As a tenant she could not get a loan because she was not an owner.

I was running my own training business by then. I wanted to help. So how could I? We had a big family, so there was no spare cash. Clearly, lots of thinking and discussions over coffee was required.

The house was £16,000, an incredibly low price even for the 1980s.

We knew that once she was a homeowner, not a tenant, she could get a loan.

And then the solution arrived. I made a suggestion: "What if I use my credit cards to buy it for you? You can then be an owner and obtain a loan, and pay me when your loan comes through."

The purchase was set in motion. When the solicitor was ready to complete the final stages, off I trundled to his offices, ready to pay. "Is it cheque or bank transfer?" he asked.

"Three credit cards," I replied.

A stunned silence followed.

He frowned. "Hmm, not sure we can do that."

"Yes you can, I'm sure. £5000 off each of these two, plus £6000 off the other one. The same as using a loan from the bank, I think."

How could he refuse?

He huffed. "We will have to charge you the credit card fees as well."

I shrugged. "That's fine."

So, there it was. Margy and my grandsons owned the house, and she paid me back as soon as her loan money came through, as planned.

The final words were from my grandson.

"Wow, Nanny! Fancy having credit cards with that much money on them!"

Bless him.

My Wild Ride, Literally
Jana Greco-Crawford

Jana Greco-Crawford loves hearing about and celebrating, the accomplishments of her fellow sisters, and is in awe over those who take great risks and put themselves out there. Shifting from a career in business, including the role of VP of Marketing, Jana became a schoolteacher and taught for twenty-five years. Newly retired, she is finding it amazing to have the freedom to do whatever she wishes. She's published a book, working on a second and endeavoring to begin a business in the area of her passion: emotional intelligence.

It was about three decades ago in the Dominican Republic. I was there with friends, and we decided to go on this horseback riding excursion. There were five of us when we arrived, then twenty more people were assigned to our group. A Dominican gentleman helped us onto the horses and started explaining that he would not be coming along. He told us his horses knew the way. One lady didn't feel safe, so she started begging him to come with us. He proceeded to tell us that he had eaten something that didn't agree with him; he needed a restroom. At that moment, one of the horses started plopping all over the place.

One of my girlfriends and I started laughing up a storm. Nothing to be proud of, but there was something about the guy telling us he had "to go" rather quickly, and the horse pooping like crazy, right on cue! As we were roaring in uncontrollable laughter, the gentleman smacked the lead horse on the bottom then disappeared. That sparked all of the horses to take off... and the Wild Ride began!

These horses didn't walk, they didn't stroll, they didn't trot, and they didn't canter—I'm not even sure gallop describes it well enough. They RAN, and incredibly fast! My friend and I weren't ready for it. We had been laughing so hard, the quick takeoff took us by surprise. We were laughing so hard we could barely hold onto the reins; we were lucky we didn't fall off.

Anyway, these horses took off up this enormously steep mountain. Tree branches and everything else smacked us in the face the entire time until we got to the peak. First, I had tears in my eyes from laughing, and then branches in them from riding. But it wasn't over.

The horses then ran down the mountain just as fast as they ran up it. They continued to race, an unbelievable pace, through bodies of water, and as all of this was going down, I was desperately trying to concentrate on holding on, while still laughing. My friend was now screaming the "F" word at the top of her lungs. Now and then, she interjected her stream of "Fs" with, "This sucks." It literally WAS a "Wild Ride." None of the riders was prepared for that kind of speed.

I laughed the entire time, while simultaneously thinking, "Holy crap, this is going to kill me." As someone who has ridden horses numerous times, I can honestly tell you that excursion was the most adventurous, thrilling, heart-pounding, risk-taking ride of my life!

MY PIECE OF WISDOM TO OTHERS IS THIS...

Just as we know that the timing of humour is everything, we also have to pay attention to the timing of laughter. I picked the wrong time to lose my mind in laughter and, as a result, almost flew off my horse quite a few times.

WORDS TO LIVE BY

"My family has very strong women. My mother never laughed at my dream of Africa, even though everyone else did because we didn't have any money, because Africa was the 'dark' continent, and because I was a girl."

–Jane Goodall, world's foremost expert on chimpanzees and environmental activist

ARRANGED ESTRANGEMENTS

Marie Beswick-Arthur

British born, Canadian raised, now living in Mexico, Marie Beswick-Arthur embraces goodness as her faith and believes learning is a lifetime pursuit. Her philosophy is to always come from a place of love, that everything is story, and story alters lives. Mother to an eclectic collection of humans, she gravitates to serving others in her role as an editor and ghostwriter as a literary concierge.

It was the kind of lesson that squeezes the fragile heart of an adult in midlife. I'd like to have learned it earlier. Grateful I know it now.

Delivered to me by my daughter, an intelligent, creative human who courageously emailed: "Can we talk?"

"Mom, when you tell me the struggles of other family members, it impacts my ability to develop an unbiased relationship with them. It influences my connections with their acquaintances and loved ones." Her voice over the phone was even.

My soul messaged me instantly; she was right. Sophisticated in her presentation, I translated: when you talk about people it affects me, please don't, here's why. I stopped in my tracks.

Over the next few days, I landed smack in a childhood memory of disliking an aunt and her son; my father's opinion had become my truth. Incidentally, that cousin and I had recently developed an amazing relationship. We had agreed our "not knowing each other sooner" was like the opposite of an arranged marriage. It was an arranged estrangement.

While I suspect my father's reason, out of insecurity, was a his family against his in-laws power play, I recognized my own insecure reasons of talking about others were an attempt to create a closeness with my daughter. How could I think that bringing up the issues of someone else was a relationship builder?

In a "show your work," I explained to my daughter that, yes, I could now see that the sharing of my perception of a family member's issues had seriously damaged her opportunity to create her own relationship with that person, denied her an opportunity to make her own meaning. I apologized. The damage was done. I could not undo what I'd said. I could, in future, check my insecurity and oversharing at the door.

I put it into my own lesson book. Negative oversharing begins innocently when, on a particularly cloudy self-relationship day, we put on the heavy, woolen coat of uncensored speech.

Beware the heavy coat. It's scratchy. There are bits of old tissues in the right pocket, something sticky in the left.

Wear the heavy coat only when necessary—to clearly issue a factual statement for safety's sake. Resist the urge to keep it on.

Unchecked, we start wearing that double-breasted, triple-lined coat every day, especially when we're in front of our phone. We begin sleeping in it. Eventually, it becomes our skin.

Be grateful for courageous acts to speak authentically so as to progress; heavy, itchy coats are inadvisable.

MY ADVICE...

Be aware of the consequences of negative oversharing. It's possible you dislike someone because of what you were told. You might have taught someone not to like another. It's not our job to tell others who "that neighbour" is, when that telling is a negative and involves our own struggles with that individual—or within ourselves.

WORDS TO LIVE BY

"I believe in kindness. Also in mischief. Also in singing, especially when singing is not necessarily prescribed."

–Mary Oliver, American poet

Merci Paris!

Mallori DeSalle

Mom, humorist, therapist and Oreo-sommelier, Mallori DeSalle, has long list of credentials after her name, all related to wellness. A professional speaker and trainer, she sparks curiosity in the young and young-at-heart. Her passion led her to the public health field and, as a result, she works with people all over the world, serving on the Board of Directors for the Association for Applied and Therapeutic Humor. When she isn't laughing, listening or learning, she spends time sampling Oreos from around the world with her husband of nearly twenty years and their three children. Her credentials don't impress her family, but occasionally, her corny jokes do make them laugh.

My second year of college, on a whim, my best friend and I booked a round-trip airline ticket to Paris for a weekend for only $99. Because this was before hotels.com or any other Internet travel booking, we arrived with no place to stay and little knowledge of the language. We managed to find an inexpensive youth hostel and ended up sharing a room with a lovely woman from Argentina.

Having only a few francs, we shopped wisely and, to keep the food fresh, we proceeded to hang our groceries (cheese, baguettes, fruit) out of our room's window in the brisk February Parisian air. After having seen the Mona Lisa and deciding there was much too significant of a fuss over a very small portrait at the Louvre, my friend and I did what any nineteen-year-old girls would do in Paris. We met boys. Instead of taking in the historic sites of Notre Dame (it cost money to go inside, after all), or spending time walking down the beautiful Champs-Élysées, we went to a karate tournament at Cité internationale universitaire de Paris (known as Cité U or the University of Paris).

This free event allowed us to experience a collegiate competition, an international campus, a new sport (outside of the *Karate Kid* movie, we had never seen karate in person) and be youthful dreamers watching adorable co-eds from another French college compete. We never did figure out who won, but we did cheer loudly.

We returned to our small women's college in southern Missouri after only two days in the iconic French city. We often relish our memories by saying, "Remember that time we went to Paris for the weekend?" People laugh, assuming this is such a foolish and impossible trip. We always wink at one another. We know it was foolish! And the impossibility of it made it that much more amazing to recount. Merci, Paris!

THE LESSON...

Take risks. The end result is worth it even if the trip takes you to unexpected places.

MY WILD RIDE
Norma Wark

Norma Wark is a farm girl at heart. Her career has been in emergency services—fire, ambulance, police support. Now retired, she loves to be outdoors with her pretty puppy, Tara, or riding her horse, Cochise. Her love of animals has led to her new passion: pet and house sitting.

I have had my Wild Ride through life. In fact, more than once in the saddle. But falling off never discouraged me from getting back on.

What a thrill to ride across a lush green meadow, forge a stream or crisscross to the mountain tops on a beautiful horse that is calm, dependable and experienced on trail rides. One feels on top of the world while scanning the beauty of nature.

But Wild Rides are not always pleasant or enjoyable, as I found out a few years ago when diagnosed with that dreadful disease, cancer. All the unknowns of future days ahead left me scared, apprehensive and sad until my attitude changed with the help of positive conversation and prayer.

After surgery and treatment, I went back to the mountaintop and saw life with a new appreciation of the beauty around me: friends, nature, everyday activities.

MY ONE PIECE OF ADVICE...

Keep on the sunny side of life...when you fall, get back up. Stay in the saddle until you are released from the cares of this world.

WORDS TO LIVE BY

"I don't need a certain number of friends; I need a number of friends I can be certain of."

–Alice Walker, novelist and poet

WORTH THE WAIT

Angie Robinson

Angie Robinson is a retired social worker and laughter yoga teacher. "Gaga" to her grandchildren, she loves to laugh and has an affinity for flamingos. She has been heard to say, "Yes, I am that crazy flamingo lady!"

I told my daughter a number of times not to make me a grandma before I was 50. Well, she didn't get married till her mid-thirties; I thought I was never going to have grandchildren.

Several years later, she handed me a small, framed picture of a raspberry. The little frame had a few baby-related etchings. It took a minute for me to register that she was pregnant: the raspberry related to the size of the fetus at that time. I could hardly contain my excitement.

I now have two handsome grandsons. Good and wonderful things are worth the wait.

ADVICE TO MY YOUNGER SELF...

It is never too late to find happiness.

Slow down and enjoy the ride.

WORDS TO LIVE BY

"There's power in allowing yourself to be known and heard, in owning your unique story, in using your authentic voice."

–Michelle Obama

FROM RUSSIA WITH(OUT) LOVE
Mary K. Lorfink-Crawford

Mary K. Crawford-Lorfink has been published in *WINK: Writers in the Know* magazine and other publications. She graduated with a BA in English from the U of MN, is an ongoing student at The Loft Literary Center, Minneapolis, MN, and a member of WOW, Women of Words. "Writing is a mystical experience, turning wonder into story."

A generation ago, I would have been one of those misunderstood eccentrics squirreling away money in my mattress with the sole intention of living outside the banking system.

But it was 2010, and although I was using Microsoft Word to pursue my interest in creative writing, I would not, under any circumstances, bank online. A nagging fear of the vast and growing Internet haunted me.

One spring day, as I was adding the final flourish to a cheery poem, my computer screen froze. Flashing across the screen was a phone number and message instructing me to contact Microsoft.

"Oh, good," I thought. "Thank you, Bill Gates!"

The technician that answered my call spoke with a Russian accent, but had the helpful, soothing tones of a dear friend eager to restore my computer's functioning. After providing him with my password, he took over my computer. As I held my hands motionless above the keyboard, I observed the technician remotely navigate the black pointer arrow across my computer screen. The bobbing arrow pointed and selected various files from my directory as the technician explained this is how he would "fix it."

Patiently optimistic, I waited and watched for several minutes, conversing with the technician as he told me to "stand by." Suddenly, my computer buzzed and screamed like a banshee then crashed. In an instant, I was disconnected from the technician. Perplexed and disheartened, I considered when and where I might take my computer in for repair. Later that day, the local news channel warned of "hackers posing as Microsoft technicians who take over your computer to download personal and financial information." Thankfully they got a big fat nothing from me. No personal or financial information on my computer! Later I thought, with a smile, *Someone in Russia finally read my poetry!*

ADVICE TO MY YOUNGER SELF...

Although hackers could have posed a threat to my financial well-being on this bright spring day, some good came of it. After a few deep breaths (of relief, I might add), I chose to install a well-known anti-virus on my computer; I no longer respond to suspicious or unknown emails; and I now had the benefit of sharing this story to enlighten others—with that punchline of an ending! Handling difficulties and learning from past mistakes teach us coping skills to call upon next time a difficult situation arises. We can emerge from our trials stronger and wiser.

CHRISTMAS MAGIC
Diane Dique

An educator and "salmon hunter," Diane Dique, has said the most rewarding aspect of her career focused on early child development and education. When she hears or reads a sad story involving children and young adults, Diane remembers the strong women in her life who loved and guided her, even though she was a challenging youngster, rebellious teenager and strong-willed young woman. Diane is forever grateful.

As our two sons got older, it got trickier each year to keep Santa's magic alive. There was always a half glass of milk left beside the hearth and cookie crumbs on the carpet. In the fireplace itself, we made sure there were bits of chewed carrots from messy reindeer peeking into the chimney.

When the boys told us they'd heard from other kids that there was no Santa Claus, we knew the game was almost up; the boys decided to put their parents to the test!

They desperately wanted a specific snow racer. We scoffed at the very idea, too dangerous, too big for Santa's sleigh and just not a good idea. We didn't think anyone should ride something like that. Besides, we reminded them, they already had crazy carpets and a toboggan. "Well, we're gonna ask Santa anyways." Off went two handwritten letters to the man in the red suit!

Lo and behold, on Christmas morning there were two of the darn things in front of the tree. We parents were shocked that Santa could manage to bring such gifts, especially if he knew how we'd feel about it! We told the boys, that Santa's elves must have been on another assignment and didn't hear our concerns.

The boys were thrilled. And, as predicted, it was Santa's last magical visit. As young adults, they have talked and laughed about Christmas, how their parents connived over the years.

But this is still one of their favourite memories.

ADVICE TO MY YOUNGER SELF...

Don't give up. You are good, you are kind and yes, you can. Search out help when you need it. Remember to forgive and never forget to laugh.

WORDS TO LIVE BY

"Is there anything better than making a kid laugh?"

–Michelle Williams, actor

ELLWOOD, LEARNING LOVE
Elspeth Crawford

Elspeth Crawford has had a variety of careers all fed by love and curiosity and connection to others. A lover of the world—its flora, fauna and people—she thinks of herself as a true scientist, steeped in wondering. Elspeth is filled with compassion for others and grateful to all those who raised her consciousness as she was growing up.

Ellwood the cat caught a claw somehow, ripped it from his paw. The vet provided painkillers and a hood to stop his harsh tongue licking the injury. After a week, the expensive painkillers were done; Ellwood was so thin he could pull the hood off his skinny head, and white bone was showing through the injury site and black hair.

I stood on the scales with him; calculated that a quarter baby aspirin would suffice and could be hidden in a piece of tuna fish. I bought a pack of circular finger bandages and some anti-bacterial cream. I sat on the kitchen floor, Ellwood jammed between my thighs, squeezed cream on the bandage, put the paw in, wrapped the lot with cotton and tied it round his body. He got it off in about two hours. So, I did it again. Then again.

The first day, he fought relentlessly, fighting the thigh prison and the bandages. I still have the marks. Then, in the night, I was wakened by a bloody paw on my face, and bloody bandage trailed across the pillow. When I headed for the kitchen surgery, Ellwood came to my lap and held up his paw. He had tears mixed in with his next creamy foot tube. Twice that night I woke. In the morning he swallowed the doctored tuna, and the times between rebandaging became blessedly longer. Within a week he had an appetite, and the bone could no longer be seen. He put his sore paw to the floor, tried walking a few steps, before reverting to the three-paw run. Six weeks later, he had recovered completely, and I knew for certain that cats can learn and love.

What I feel about this is very simple. First, I want to weep when I remember how he fought, then learned to trust me, through the hurting. He soon came every time the bandage was off and, even though he jerked or whimpered as I replaced it, he never again clawed me to free himself.

I came to see that care, about which we often talk, is nothing more than relentless attention to whatever it is that is needed. After a while, it lets up, or it does not. We may have the resources of time and space to give that care, or we may not. Caring for Ellwood and his paw was no different from caring for a tiny baby or for my friend before she died, though the nurses in hospice did more of that than I did.

We hope our care will bring about a change; if it does not, or cannot, we grieve. This idea of care was what turned me into an activist. Cruelty exists, pain exists, exploitation in this world of inequity exists. I despair when white supremacy and economic injustice leave little room for care. If I can lessen pain for anyone—or a cat—I care and try. Unexpectedly, gratitude arrives. Like Ellwood, I have energy to live and love.

MY FAVOURITE QUOTE...

"Those who seek new land have to spend a long time out of sight of the shore."

–Andre Gide

MY ADVICE...

Who am I to give advice? I like to have conversations, engage people. I don't know anyone's backstory, so I try to hear what they know, how they are, what sort of things they want to do. If I don't like it, I say so, with respect and compassion as far as I can. If I do like it, great. Either way, conversations manage to get some kind of connection. I guess my advice is: try it.

In Pursuit of a Dream

Janice Kimball

Janice Kimball, author, visual artist and retired university instructor, was born in Detroit, Michigan. Her paintings, sculpture and printmaking are in the permanent collections of the Henry Ford Library, The Ukrainian Museum of Contemporary Art and Columbia College, Chicago, and are housed in other institutions. She has the distinction as the only American painter awarded a medal by The National Camera de Commercial in Guadalajara, Mexico. "I come from a heritage of abused women. My third and latest book, SWOBODA'S HIDDEN WOMEN, is a family memoir beginning in 18th century Austria and ending in Detroit, Michigan, in 1963 when I was 23 years old and began to plan my escape."

I was not yet sixty when I moved from Detroit to the highlands of central Mexico to escape old hopes and expectations. There, along with my ravenous former street dog, Dulce, and a cat I had been in love with until he ate my cockatoo, I came to live an idyllic life. The only thing missing was a man.

Having not yet learned that you can't find love by searching,
I went out in pursuit of it. My small truck bounced down the
cobblestone streets that led to Avenue Pepe Guizar where I was to
turn left at the traffic light. My goal was the California
Restaurant, sure to be filled with expatriates getting in touch with
their souls while eating turkey dinner, the restaurant's Thursday
special.

My elbow leaned out the window as I waited for the light to turn
green. My dream man rode up on his horse alongside me, his
steed prancing to the Mariachi music that played on my radio. He
tipped his sombrero and blew me a kiss. Our eyes locked in
dreamy contemplation. In a slow stride we made the left-hand
turn together. I wanted the moment to last forever, but fate
intervened with the sound of a beeping horn behind us. This
startled the charro's steed, and they galloped off, making a quick
turn onto the street that led to the back entrance of the bull ring.

Surely my man wasn't gone forever, I thought later, chewing on
a slice of turkey thigh at the California, although I had ordered
white meat. And wouldn't my dream-man have passed Tom's
restaurant? It often sold draft beer to Charros who left their horses
tied to a tree out front. Perhaps that was the place we were meant
to meet. But there would be no magic in that.

It was an unlikely dream that his steed would pull up beside me at
our intersection on the following Friday. As I sat at the red light,
finally ready to give up, a dog with long legs strode up beside me,
panting. Why, that dog is the spitting image of Dulce, I thought.
He jumped up and stuck his head though the window. I recoiled
as unwelcome saliva from the dog's dripping tongue ran down my
leg. It was then that I realized that indeed it was Dulce. I opened
the door before the light turned green, and he jumped in.

His snoring at the foot of the bed that night woke me, so I got up
to get a cookie. Dulce rose too, as he had guessed my intention.
As I leaned over to give him a bite, I noticed the petal of a flower

blossom hanging from a hair of his lower lip. I hated it when he ate the Azaleas, yet smiled when I reflected on the magic in my life. After all, I didn't need to have a man to fall in love. I knew that for sure because I had fallen in love with Mexico.

ADVICE TO MY YOUNGER SELF...

Guard who you were meant to be, lest it be stolen from you. Believe in Miracles.

WORDS TO LIVE BY

"Nothing is worth more than laughter. It is strength to laugh and to abandon oneself, to be light."

–Frida Kahlo, 20th-century Mexican painter

Always Look Your Best!

Joyce Faye Young-Riggs

Joyce Faye Young-Riggs was born in Valdosta, Georgia, in 1928. She moved to Atlanta after high school and met her husband, Sam, at a church gathering. They were married in 1951 and had a daughter and two sons. The family lived in Clearwater, Florida, for eight years. Faye enjoyed cooking, baking, decorating, playing bridge, entertaining and playing golf. Ten years after Sam passed away, she remarried at age 80. Faye lives in assisted living in the Atlanta area near her family. She has six grandchildren and six great-grandchildren.

Mother, who is almost 92, has always been a very fashionable dresser, loves shoes and nice jewelry. She always had a good eye for fashion and color and, to this day, is careful to dress in style. She sometimes will get to talking about her eventual passing and has told my brothers and I that we are to tell only funny stories at her funeral.

That, of course, got us dividing up the funny stories among ourselves and who would tell what. Mom got a big kick out of our conversation, and it also got her off the subject of her death

(I thought). As our discussion was coming to an end, however, Mom told us she had one more thing she wanted us to do. "On the way to the cemetery, have the hearse swing by Talbots, Chicos, Globe Shoes and Levy Jewelers so they can take a look and make sure I am dressed and accessorized appropriately!"

Of Mom...When In Italy...

My brother, a career Army physician, was stationed near Pisa, Italy, in the 1980s. Mom, Dad and I spent several weeks visiting during his assignment there.

A couple of weeks into our visit Mom lamented that she had been in Italy for two weeks and had not yet been pinched!

A few days later, we took a trip to Florence. While walking down the Ponte Vecchio, Mom and I leading the group, she suddenly yelped!

"What happened?" I asked.

"Someone just pinched me!" Mom exclaimed.

We both turned just in time to see Dad step up on the opposite curb and roar with laughter. He, as always, was very good about making sure Mom got what she wanted.

MY ADVICE...

Faye continues to be dedicated and serious about supporting local businesses. Shop in your local community when you can; join the church in your neighborhood when it makes sense; support local charities. This civic support not only helps your neighbours but uplifts the community and helps you get to know those who live around you.

Surrounded by Story Retreat
Breakout Room Two

- Is it a little exhilarating to jot your jottables in the margins?

- If you haven't, have you been tempted?

- Have you smiled while your pen was moving across the page?

- Has a tear or two formed when your pen had to stop on a page?

- Do you already have a blank book on the side or in mind for later use?

A checkmark for "Yes" beside any of the above indicates you are in the right place at the perfect retreat for you. Two yeses suggest you have the potential to become a serial journaler. Three, and there might be a memoirist waiting to leap out of you. Four or five? There's no stopping you.

You are now ready to enter ROOM TWO of your retreat.

Now that you have read the first 36 stories, I wonder about your responses. Are you recalling a particular story that could have fit into this collection? If so, in a few words, can you jot a reminder in the margin in case you want to expand on it later?

Completing this book with your own thoughts will certainly lead you on a creative adventure. Who knows? There might be an anthology in you. Perhaps a memoirist is eager to emerge. Maybe a poet resides in your soul. For now, allow your memories to lead you to your own unique stories. Through this, creativity will flow.

Your stories are every bit as worthy as the submissions received and printed. Every word, phrase, doodle that you add to these journaling pages becomes a reflection of you...the authentic you. You, without labels or roles or situations. You, existing in the timelessness that writing provides.

Stories help us to understand our lives. They connect us with others, and their creative energy allows us to pass along important family values to others.

Are you noticing the relationship between negative and positive experiences as you recall your memories?

When we experience a happy event, we tend to overestimate how often we will recall it in the future. We think that we will remember it forever. Sadly, the distractions of everyday life intervene, and we simply forget to remember.

Savour your memories by engaging in the following tips so that current and future happy events are better remembered:

1. Live in the moment. Often we are so busy capturing the perfect shot, running to control details, thinking about how we got here, thinking about how much time until we leave, that we forget our visit to New York because we really weren't in New York. We forget to notice the people, the smells, the sounds and the wonders all around.

2. Choose to practice recalling happy times. A regular dinner with friends to reminisce about the special reunion event or writing in a gratitude journal can reap lasting benefits.

3. Sleep is important for memory. During deep sleep, memories are encoded for future recall.

4. Identify peak experiences/important events that you want to recall. The first journaling page in this Breakout Room offers suggestions for encoding a positive memory and improving recall in the future.

5. Use your feel-good memories to inform the future…but be attentive to living in the present.

Source: Launch Project, August 4, 2017, Keep Happy Memories from Fading Fast. www.yourlaunchproject.com

THE POWER OF RECALL

Recalling painful moments does, in a way, keep us out of future harm. Too much negative recall can stop us from experiencing life's adventures. Strategies to retain the positive happy-place moments include using all your senses to infuse good memories with detail. Suggested steps:

1. Think of a recent positive experience.

2. Engage all your senses as you move the memory around in your mind.

3. Where were you? What do you see? How do you feel?

4. If there was another person involved, or people, can you see their face(s)? What were they wearing? How do you think they were feeling? Why do you think they were feeling that way?

5. What can you hear? What can you smell? Is there a touch associated with this memory?

6. What is the strongest, most positive part of this memory?

7. Stop for a moment and bathe in the details. Occasionally reviewing the memory in this way can keep it fresh and accessible. Positive memories awaken positive emotions which encourages well-being.

Can you recall three positive memories?

Use the above technique in recall, then write like no one is watching. Remember putting down the details is more powerful than thinking the thoughts.

AN ODE TO GRATITUDE

Gratitude is an attitude we choose, but where does it come from? How does it develop in us? When I think of gratitude, my mind chooses this memory:

When I was six, my parents moved our family from the farm to a village of 250 people. Up to that point, our extended family had provided most of my social experiences, so I went to school a shy but curious child.

As I was walking to school by myself, I noticed my older brother walking a block ahead with a young man who I knew was in grade twelve and, therefore, in my mind, worthy of adulation. As I watched, I saw a piece of paper flutter out of the older boy's pocket, and I ran to pick it up before the wind blew it away. Cautiously, I tapped on his back to get his attention and then held out the paper money to him. With a big smile, he turned, looked down at me, took the large bill, exchanged it for a dollar bill, bent down, folded it in my hand, and sincerely said, "Thank you very much."

I felt like the clouds parted, the sun shone brighter and I had been given the world. I had never had anyone give me a whole dollar bill for myself. More importantly, even though I was this little kid, I felt acknowledged and supremely validated. It was a good feeling and I believe planted within me a seed of generosity and gratitude.

I'm reminded that someone anonymous but wise said, "You never know what part of the presentation makes the sale." Who would have thought that a chance event would have lifelong impact on a little girl?

Beyond learning please and thank you as a child, is there an incident that served as an example of gratitude in your life?

How do you show your gratitude?

To find out—and discover steps for promoting even more gratitude in your life—take the quiz at the resource listed below. It's based on a quick, twenty-question scale developed by psychologists Mitchel Adler and Nancy Fagley.* Note any surprises from the results.

* Find quizzes at Greater Good Science Center:

https://greatergood.berkeley.edu/quizzes/take_quiz/gratitude

GIFTS ALL AROUND

When an occasion arises that requires a gift, how do you choose it? Is it a random choice, something to fill the need of the recipient, or is it a feeling/message/value that you want to share?

Think of a gift that you have given that brought you the most pleasure (to give).

Consider the gifts that you have received...which one was your favourite?

On a First Name Basis

Please print your first name here. S-l-o-w-l-y. Feel each letter.

Were you named after a family member or someone famous? If so, do you feel a familiarity with that person? What is the story about your first name? If there isn't a story, can you create one?

If there is a shortened version of your name what is it?

If you are known by a nickname, what is that name and the story behind it?

If you were to choose a new name for yourself, what would it be? Why?

Inspired by: Wiser Now Wednesday www.wisernow.com
Kathy Laurenhue

I Love Quotations

Of these three quotations, circle the one that resonates with you?

"You can't be that kid standing at the top of the waterslide overthinking it. You have to go down the chute."

–Tina Fey

"I wanted a perfect ending. Now I've learned, the hard way, that some poems don't rhyme and some stories don't have a clear beginning, middle and end. Life is about not knowing, having to change, taking the moment and making the best of it, without knowing what's going to happen next."

–Gilda Radner, Delicious Ambiguity

"Be Who You Are and Say What You Feel Because Those Who Mind Don't Matter and Those Who Matter Don't Mind."

–Dr. Seuss

What kind of quotation has meaning for you? Funny, inspirational, thoughtful, practical or other? Note any you know or sort-of know by heart.

Do you have a phrase that you often repeat that could be part of your motto or your own quotation?

If you were going to write five words that represent the most important values or beliefs of your life, which ones would they be?

Create a quotation of your own.

Here's your chance to speak to the world; to have something go viral.

THE CLEANEST CLOSET

If you were to clean out your closet and nakedness was not an issue, which two items would you keep and why? How long have they been in your closet? Did you choose them or were they a gift?

Tell the page the story of your relationship with these keepers:

There Will Be Days Like This

"There'll be days like this," my momma said.

When you open your hands to catch and wind up with only blisters and bruises. When you step out of the phone booth and try to fly, and the very people you want to save are the ones standing on your cape.

When your boots will fill with rain, and you'll be up to your knees with disappointment.

And those are the very days you have all the more reason to say, "Thank you."

–Sarah Kay, poet, performer, educator and
the founder of Project VOICE.

Share a day when you tried so hard, and the results of your efforts were disappointing or even worse. Were there some moments of clarity that turned the experience toward the positive?

I LOVE HATS

I love the funny ones made from newspaper, my mom's pillbox covered with white daisies, the fascinator made of feathers, the slouch hat of cork that I had to buy in Portugal. My closet collects them. I aspire to model them, though other than the beach, rarely find an occasion to wear one.

Do you have a bevy of similar items collected for your personal pleasure? What are your favorites?

Is there a crazy collector in your life? Share about that person. Is it you? Share even more.

You Won!

Imagine that you have just won the grand prize at the Home Show. You will receive a fully furnished dream home of your choice…complete with the services of a decorator.

What choices would you make? Picket fence or pool? What colors would you use inside your new home? Describe the area that you would use as your special sanctuary? Who would be invited to your first barbecue?

LASSIE OR MISS ARISTO-CAT

Are you an animal lover? Dogs, cats, horses, budgie, gecko? If you had a pet or pets as a child, share your memories. If you didn't have one and wanted one, what was that like. Describe your best life with the perfect pet.

A ROOM WITH YOUR VIEW

A ROOM WITH YOUR VIEW

3

GRATITUDE

Keynote: Gratitude

Highlights

- A happy, mentally healthy brain regularly recalls positive memories

- Gratitude is associated with all forms of happiness

- When we experience gratitude—giving or receiving—the brain releases mood-enhancing chemicals

- Gratitude requires a conscious choice

- Gratitude practice involves paying attention to gifts received

- It's easy to be grateful for the good things in life

- Being grateful for sorrows and life lessons involves a deeper insight

Heartwarming stories that beg to be retold come from a positive view of life and a deep sense of gratitude—both qualities are part of human nature.

Gratitude in all forms is associated with happiness. A happy, mentally healthy brain is one that regularly recalls positive moments and feelings of gratitude. Whether we say thank you to someone or receive thanks from others, it brings pure satisfaction and encourages reciprocity.

The late devotional writer and psychologist, Henri Nouwen, offers two quotations about the importance of gratitude:

"Gratitude as a discipline involves a conscious choice. I can choose to be grateful even when my emotions and feelings are hurt and resentful."

Nouwen further clarified that the ability to live gratefully doesn't always come naturally or easily.

> "To be grateful for the good things that happen in our lives is easy, but to be grateful for all of our lives—the good as well as the bad, the moments of joy as well as the moments of sorrow, the successes as well as the failures, the rewards as well as the rejections—that requires hard work. We are only truly grateful people when we can say thank you to all that has brought us to the present moment."

When we express gratitude and receive the same, our brain releases dopamine and serotonin, the two crucial neurotransmitters responsible for our emotions, and they make us feel good. They enhance our mood immediately, making us feel happy from the inside. Consciously cultivating an attitude of gratitude builds up a sort of psychological immune system that can cushion us when we fall.

One of the first steps in gratitude practice is to pay attention to what is going right in life and actively recognize the positive contributions that others make. Systematically recording blessings—translating thoughts into words—has advantages over just thinking the thoughts. It is suggested that gratitude journaling and writing gratitude letters can promote humility, resilience and help us to appreciate others.

A starting point in establishing a gratitude practice could look like this:

Focus on the gifts you have received in life; simple everyday pleasures: your warm blanket, the adoration in your puppy's eyes, the sky at dawn, people in your life or gestures of kindness from others. We might not normally think about these things as gifts, but take a moment to really savor them, think about their value and then write them out every night before going to sleep.

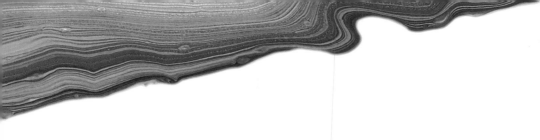

On Officially Becoming an Old Woman
Antonia Gossner

Antonia Gossner is a 75-year-old, recently widowed woman just beginning to contemplate the possibilities of a life without the responsibilities of employment or caregiving. She is relishing being the grandmother she always longed to be, always available, always delighted to welcome a grandchild...or two or more. She looks forward to discovering and deciding on new goals, whatever they may be.

I am now officially an Old Woman. Wait staff call me "dear" and later, chirp to one another, "Isn't she cute?" Cashiers are taken aback when I refuse their offers to carry my groceries, toting away my veggies and my ten-kilogram bag of flour on my own. I myself, catching an unexpected glimpse of my reflection in a mirror in a mall, am, for a moment, taken by surprise. "Who is that familiar-looking old woman?"

The girl-child who lives inside my head, the true me, is by turns astonished and amused. She knows that I walk far more than the current requisite number of steps each day, that I plank regularly, that I pray, meditate, read and garden. She knows that I am not dead yet.

Time, if we are given enough of it, plays a huge practical joke on us. The body ages, hair turns grey, wrinkles appear, skin sags. In a culture obsessed with youth and beauty, the Old Woman becomes invisible. Yet the joke is turned back on Time; her spirit remains strong and vibrant, inquisitive and capable. No longer fettered by the responsibilities and expectations that rule the life of a Young Woman, I am, for the first time in my life, free to please myself. I can choose to cook or not, to watch television in bed while eating chocolate cake, to doze in a hammock throughout a sunlit afternoon. I can stay home and read and need not explain myself to anyone.

Happily, the cloak of invisibility is powerless over dogs, cats, small children and old friends. These are able to see me clearly, and they provide love and touch, acceptance and connection.

Yes, I am officially an Old Woman, and that is officially a very good thing to be.

MY ONE PIECE OF ADVICE...

Extend to your own failings the same acceptance and understanding that you extend to those of others.

When I Grow Up, I Want To Be a Tap-dancing Gypsy

Mary Kay Morrison

International speaker and educator who has taught at many levels of the educational spectrum, Mary Kay Morrison provides keynote presentations and programs on the neuroscience of humor. Past-president of AATH (Association of Applied and Therapeutic Humor), founder and director of the AATH Humor Academy, and 2016 AATH Lifetime Award recipient, one of her books, *Using Humor to Maximize Living*, is a notable college textbook. Her most recent book: *Legacy of Laughter: A Grandparent Guide and Playbook* was written with the contributions of her twelve brilliant grandchildren.

Several years ago, my six-year-old granddaughter brought home a beautiful self-portrait. She said that her teacher asked them to draw what they were going to be when they grew up. With great detail, my grandchild described the hat, shoes and fancy clothing that depicted a tap-dancing gypsy. I sought to clarify her goals, and, after a little discussion, she asked me what a gypsy was. When she found out that it was someone who travels lightly and even wanders from place to place, she was quite satisfied with her decision.

After quite a bit of laughter with my daughter (her mom),
I believe that I too want to be a tap-dancing gypsy when I grow
up. I love to dance and move and hope that I can always enjoy the
activity that comes to express joyful energy. I also know it is
a powerful way to keep the brain engaged when the body
is moving and active. So, the tap-dancing sounds like something
that I would like to try.

Traveling like a gypsy and wandering around in a rather random
pattern is a way that my husband and I like to travel. It is
energizing to find adventure in far-away places and meet diverse
folks. Our favorite travel experiences have come from chatting
with random strangers along the way. We ask for
recommendations of unique regional hideaways and historic
information. Of course, we do not leave without asking about
their favorite hometown restaurant.

In my book, *Using Humor to Maximize Living*, and on my
Humor Quest website, I share the research on the health benefits
of laughter and humor. Play is a trigger for laughter and delight.
It is critically important for optimal brain development not only
for children, but for adults. Joyful play is essential for lifelong
learning with humergy, which is the energy that comes from
optimism, joy and humour. My goal is to find playful activities
that bring laughter and delight in every day.

That is why my six-year-old granddaughter's goal seems perfect
for me. I really never do want to grow up. I want to continue to
do cartwheels, swing whenever possible and practice the hula-
hoop. Becoming a tap-dancing gypsy sounds like a perfect way to
optimize my golden years.

ADVICE FOR MY YOUNGER SELF...

Take tap dancing lessons! And, of course, play every day.

Not So Missing Person
Linda J. Pedley

When author and illustrator, Linda J. Pedley, felt she needed more to fulfill her journey as a writer, she established a publishing company in 2010 to help others become published authors. Her motto is learn, share and create; she actively advocates people share what they know and encourages lifetime learning.

The events were almost forty years apart and for reasons unalike. Both happened in the mountains—whether there is some connection with that significance, I don't know. I just know it's the place where I can find myself these days. Back then, it was where I found someone else.

In September 1980, I was road tripping with a friend. It was a time of dining, drinking and dancing until all hours of the morning. I was looking for love—apparently, in all the wrong places, like the song says. My find that night ticked all the right boxes, so I ditched my road-trip friend and left with the new find: him.

By morning, my friend had frantically called the RCMP only to be informed I was not yet officially a missing person.

Fast forward to 2014. Looking for love has morphed into finding myself and filling the soul with good things. The mountains and wild horses call. But it is also a time when communication has created a world where contact is instantaneous, and we can demand immediacy. At any given time, within moments, we can know where someone is or be close to locating them. This translates to an ease, and even a habit, of staying in touch unless you meet the limits of today's devices—reception.

It just so happens I was out of reception for too long (24 hours), and that prompted a call by my friend and my daughter. Upon my return from exploring the backroads to the B&B where I stayed, I discovered the RCMP were inquiring into my whereabouts. I promptly contacted home to assure everyone I was okay.

Of course, no one intended to intrude on my privacy. It was incredible to know that people love me enough to check on me. But our easy-to-always-be-connected world encroaches on the private spaces that we crave to find the self.

What I do know is I am truly thankful my experiences never resulted in harmful outcomes. I am certainly blessed to have such a caring daughter and friend. I am also happy to have the memories of those times when I "disappeared" to find myself.

ADVICE TO MY YOUNGER SELF...

Always consider the impact of your actions on others.

My Story
Patti Heerhartz

Executive Director of several California Governor's Advisory Boards and a salmon hunter, Patti Heerhartz is a dedicated volunteer with a unique agency called Petal Connection. She has shared it's her favorite part of the week when she and other members design simple bedside floral bouquets for those in hospice or nursing homes. Otherwise discarded as excess, these flower donations from grocery stores and florists make thousands of bouquets each year.

When I was a college senior, several of my friends were hired by an international charter airline. This sounded way more fun than school, so on a whim I decided to apply as well. My friends advised me that the airline preferred a second language although they did not test for it, so I fibbed and said I spoke French. (Took two years of French in high school and flunked the second year.)

Much to my parents' chagrin, I accepted the job, quit school and went to work flying all over the world. Most trips were military charters taking troops in and out of Vietnam. I thought nighttime mortar fire and going into very dangerous places were exciting. Besides, the layovers were in Hawaii, Japan, Thailand and Alaska.

Being one of a few American, young, single women on a usually all-male airbase was pretty good for the ego as well. I was twenty-two and fearless—aka stupid. Seriously though, it was difficult for me to deliver planeloads of troops to a war zone; bringing them home was another story—relief in knowing they would be safe. Even though they were exhausted, they appeared jubilant with relief.

One private charter, I was told that we were taking French dignitaries from Paris to London; I was to be the interpreter and give all the in-flight announcements. Upon receiving this news, I knew I would soon be fired. However, I spent the entire evening with our hotel bellman who helped me with my speech. The next day, I was a nervous wreck and muddled my way through. At the end, the group began clapping. Yes, clapping! Turns out they all spoke perfect English. But they appreciated my effort and gave me perfume and bonbons.

I NEVER regretted leaving college, although I returned later. That three-year experience was life-changing and more valuable than a traditional college education. It instilled in me a yearning for travel that has never wavered. It was truly a wild ride in every sense of the words.

LIFE LESSON TO SHARE...

Take Chances, Forgive Quickly,

Have Fun, Give Everything,

And Have No Regrets.

TWELVE TIME ZONES TO TRUE LOVE

Anna Elena Berlin

Anna Elena Berlin has been a traveler her entire life…all of which led her to be a certified life coach, researcher, writer, publisher and owner of Wisen-Up.com. She sees her purpose as uplifting people so they Feel Better, Do Better and Live Better with and through information, inspiration, encouragement and options they may not even be aware of.

The clothes I packed in my Hawaiian rental were damp from torrential rain. But I was determined to fly to Greece that day and heal my heart that had been shattered by betrayal.

I'd flown to Hawaii from Mexico seeking comforting relief from my daughter and her fiancé. They did help me feel better, as did several weeks of therapies I received staying at the Aloha Wellness Center, plus a month in a Pahoa rainforest cottage. However, as a Certified Life Coach, I knew I had to be more proactive to completely heal. So, I kept asking myself, "What do you really need?"

I remembered Greece always made me feel good. I knew that I would have my fill of traditional vegetable dishes, sunshine, turquoise seas and hopefully get a reinvigorated life. All of this and much more were only twelve time zones away...and thirty hours of travel time.

I decided to give myself a mission so that this trip would have purpose and meaning beyond just trying to pull myself together. I'd go to Kalamata to find the best organic olive oil for my chef daughter to use in her future food business, and for our family's personal health—it is a brain superfood.

First stop, though, was Agia Effimia on the gorgeous island of Kefalonia for a week of seaside introspection. Then I felt ready to meet the olive farmer in Kalamata who had arranged for me to rent his sister's Airbnb for a month.

It was perfectly situated in historic old town, and only a block away was a gym where I could regain my strength. One rainy morning, the tables were all taken inside the coffee shop I frequented before working out. Seeing my need, the man that usually sat at the table next to mine asked if I wanted to sit with him and away from smokers.

After ten days of sharing his table each morning, we started dating.

It had only been four months since my emotional trauma, and I kept telling myself, "You aren't ready for love yet." I tried repeatedly to talk myself out of falling for this handsome Greek man, fifteen years younger than me.

But that judgement flew out the window when, one evening, he asked me, "Anna, what are we doing here?"

I truthfully replied, "I don't know what you're doing, but I think I'm falling in love."

He asked, "Do you believe in true love?"

I replied, "Yes, I do."

Then he asked, "What do you think it is?"

It took me a year to truthfully answer him. By then true love had healed me completely.

Fast forward two years. Did it work out? Yes, it did! Did we get married? Yes, we did! Then Covid-19 distress caused us to get unmarried. Did that keep us from loving each other? No, it didn't...we're getting married again! Life is so interesting.

God has a much better imagination than we do; I honestly felt I was being led.

ADVICE TO MY YOUNGER SELF...

Self-knowledge is the best knowledge. It enables you to be true to yourself. You are more powerful than you know; make your choices through love, not fear. Life is long, do everything that lights up your heart. Live with integrity and always take the high road, even if it doesn't feel good. Everything in life is either worth it to you, or it's not worth it to you. Make good health and well-being your priority; they make all you do possible. Enjoy your youth; you get to be old a really long time.

Midlife Student Changes Course

Sharon Love Cook

Sharon Love Cook is a writer and cartoonist known for her *Granite Cove Mysteries.* All her books are listed at: https://tinyurl.com/y77btbas including *15 Reasons Why: Men are for Now, Cats are Forever.*

I went back to college in my forties, having been a '60s art school dropout. This time, I was bitten by the desire to help humanity, something I called the Mother Teresa Syndrome. And though I wanted to ease the world's suffering, I was also squeamish about encountering blood and bodily fluids. Thus, I decided to become a physical rehab specialist.

During my second year, students were assigned to a hospital for a two-month practicum. Starting out, I was instructed to help patients with their ADLs: activities of daily living. Every morning, I approached the beds on my ward, asking, "Would you like to brush your teeth?" When someone agreed, I'd rummage around in my ADL cart for toothbrush and toothpaste. This was easy work, until one morning an elderly patient reached into her mouth and handed me her teeth. My instructors had never mentioned this scenario.

Feeling awkward, but not wanting to appear unprofessional, I calmly slipped the teeth into the pocket of my lab coat, saying, "I'll take care of this." I'd planned to ask a helpful CNA (certified nursing assistant) regarding the proper procedure. Yet, after a long day on the unit, I forgot.

The following morning, I was reminded when I donned my lab coat and felt the weight in my right pocket. If that wasn't bad enough, I couldn't remember which patient owned the teeth. Hiding my desperation, I pushed my cart into room after room, assessing patients' mouths. If someone was sleeping, I surreptitiously peeked inside. This eventually paid off when I discovered the toothless patient. When I handed her the teeth, she slid them in, nodding her approval.

When the semester ended, I visited the college's Adult Student Services—A.S.S.—to talk about changing my major. I still wanted to help people, but in some cases I felt I was more hindrance than help. I could never learn to use the dreaded goniometer, an instrument for gauging joint movement. I was invariably a few inches off, causing nit-picking instructors to complain.

After listening to me, the A.S.S. dean asked, "Didn't I read an essay you wrote for the college newspaper?" I'd written about being a "non-trad" adult student. My classmates might hang out with me, yet they'd never invite me to go along on spring break. The dean leaned forward. "Sharon, I think you should be pursuing a writing career."

Her remark surprised me. At the same time, it made sense. I'd been a round peg, struggling to fit into a square space. With hard work and perseverance, I'd have made it, although the trek wouldn't have been a joyous one.

I changed majors and felt a burden lifted. Not only did I finish with a bachelor's degree, I completed art school as well. Sometimes, for the fun of it, I write and illustrate my stories.

I still like to help people, but now I do it outside a hospital setting.

MY ADVICE TO A YOUNGER WOMAN...

If you like to laugh, marry someone with a sense of humor.

It will help you weather the bumps in life's road.

WORDS TO LIVE BY

"For there is always light. If only we're brave enough to see it. If only we're brave enough to be it."

–Amanda Gorman, Inauguration Day Poet

THE TOWN WE CALL WELCOME

Nila Nielsen

Nila Nielsen is a native Nebraskan who loves life and enjoys the blessings that it brings: sunrises and sunsets, the beauty of the four seasons, the laughter of children, road trips with friends and spending time with family and grandchildren. She enjoyed a long career in education, starting as a teacher in a one-room country school and ending in one of the largest districts in Nebraska as an elementary principal. In retirement, Nila is thrilled to be able to serve as a volunteer, helping others learn about the benefits of humor.

On the morning of the 2019 eclipse of the sun, my daughter and I decided on a whim to travel to the nearest preferred location to view the historic moment. We packed up her three-month-old, and off we went for our first three-generation road trip.

Luckily, there was a roadside vendor who happily sold us high-quality, high-priced cardboard viewing glasses and two solar caps that we just had to have. Needless to say, we were excited. The drive would only be 90 minutes, and we were going to be a part of history.

The further we went, the more cloudy it became. As we were nearing our destination, we were being slowed by traffic and knew if we continued, we wouldn't get there in time and would have to watch from the car. Sadly, we turned around.

Twenty minutes later, since time was running out, we pulled into a small town in the middle of nowhere to find a place to stop and view the eclipse. We parked on Main Street in front of the local Legion Hall. Immediately, a woman emerged from the hall to welcome us and let us know we could come in and make ourselves at home. Another woman suggested we walk with her family down the street to a schoolyard, stating that the streetlights would soon be coming on and would hamper our view. To our amazement, the clouds began to part. For five minutes it was sunny and bright, right before the eclipse began. We put on our glasses and captured history, thanks to the kindness of those around us.

As we prepared to leave, I asked my daughter what the name of the town was. She didn't know but pointed at faded billboard across the street that said "Welcome." We both agreed that this town would always be called Welcome by us.

My one piece of advice...

Always be kind. It is easy to do and is always remembered by those who receive it. Maybe it's as simple as opening a door, sharing a smile or taking time to listen. No matter how big or small, your acts of kindness do make a difference.

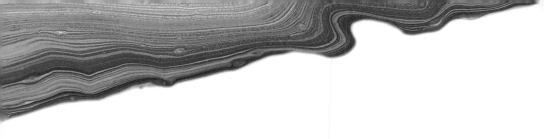

MUSINGS OF DAILY LIFE...A STANZA A DAY

Alice Armstrong

Born, educated and married in the Shetland Islands, Alice Armstrong immigrated to Canada with her family in 1962. She is a prolific writer of prose and an active member of the Writing Circle at her Lodge. When they hold their weekly Devotional Hour, they read uplifting stories, play beautiful music and ask Alice for her latest four-line poem. These days, Alice writes about her memories and daily experiences—the ladies who come to clean and the maintenance men out her window.

She wipes the door handles, windowsills and shelves,

And if that isn't enough,

Just in case the last conversation got vulgar and virile,

She wipes out the telephone's mouth.

The bathroom floor was icy cold,

The toilet seat was wet; how much worse can it get?

The light went off in the middle of my shower which would have been worse when I was young,

But now, at 83 years of age, I knew where everything hung.

When they heard of my frustration,

The maintenance men did what they do best,

They flex their massive muscles,

And heave the haven to the west.

The little boy said, read me a poem.

The little girl said, sing me a song.

Thank them both with big, happy smiles,

And they will be your favourite children all day long.

MY THOUGHT FOR THE DAY...

The Heart does not always share with the lips the thought that it treasures.

WET AND WILD SUMMER FUN

Coby Veeken

Coby Veeken lives close to nature: picking berries, swimming in the lake, gardening outdoors and tending to many indoor plants. By day, her laundry dries on clotheslines, and on winter evenings she enjoys the warmth of her wood-burning fireplace while knitting, sewing or reading. She has pondered: can we be any more earthly than with a spirituality that includes creation?

Our family looks forward to an annual canoe and camping trip every July long weekend. This particular occasion was a lovely warm summer day on the beautiful Red Deer River. Although daughter Mary-Lou knew how and what to do in a canoe, her husband Jim (paddling at the back) and I (seated in the middle)—not so much!

The adventure began with Mary-Lou showing off a bit with an eddy turn to park our canoe behind a large rock in the middle of the river. The others in the group showed surprise and laughed hilariously as they paddled past us down the river. We needed to spin out of the eddy to follow them and, in good spirits, we leaned into the turn.

It became obvious that overall our team was lighter on experience than desired! The canoe tipped and everything and every one of us ended up in the water.

Mary-Lou commanded, "Mom, get to the back of the boat!" However, I heard, "Mom, get back into the boat!" So, back into the water-filled canoe I jumped. I grabbed a bucket floating toward me and started bailing the swamped boat, while Jim and Mary-Lou pushed the canoe to the edge of the river.

By this time the whole group had gathered and joined in the fun of our adventure. Everything was retrieved, and we have a hilarious story to share...one that has been enjoyed time and again at family gatherings.

ADVICE TO MY YOUNGER SELF...

Try all kinds of outdoor activities. One does not have to be a star to enjoy life and nature.

THE BLESSING
Pat Korchinski

Pat Korchinski says she is blessed to have been born into a large family with a deep faith. She credits those strengths as having carried her through life, brought her peace in times of stress and turmoil, and sent her a wonderful man to whom she has been married for fifty years.

After my husband and I adopted our children, a boy and girl, our family was complete, or so we thought.

One year, all of my family got together to arrange a group Christmas present to send my mom and dad on a pilgrimage to Europe. On this trip, they went to Lourdes in France, where my parents lit a separate candle for each one of their fourteen children. With the candles glowing, they said a special prayer pertaining to each child.

For my husband and I, they prayed we would have a natural child. Nine months to the day, our beautiful, healthy, daughter was born.

She grew up always saying she was the miracle in the family. However, our two adopted children always told her that Mom and Dad had to take her. They didn't get a choice, whereas they were specifically chosen.

We were and are truly blessed.

MY SMALL PIECE OF ADVICE...

All we have on this earth is gift. We are called to share all of our gifts with others, and in return, we are blessed with a wonderful life.

WORDS TO LIVE BY

"I don't think about my life in terms of numbers. First of all, I ain't never gonna be old because I ain't got time to be old. I can't stop long enough to grow old."

–Dolly Parton, *The Oprah Conversation*, November 2020

WHAT MORE COULD WE WISH FOR
Mechtild Brennen

Secretary/Treasurer for a cross-country ski club, assistant cross-country ski instructor for Jackrabbits, secretary for pre-school, school volunteer, 4-H Cooking Leader, secretary for the local Quilting Guild and insulation installer for a Habitat for Humanity houses comprise some of the groups Mechtild Brennen has the pleasure to be involved with. In a hurried, self-centered world, she counts herself grateful to be a volunteer, as well as have the support of her best friend and life partner, and of their two adult children.

Volunteering has been a part of my life for a long time and started in the Netherlands in grade five, when students would go door-to-door once a year to sell Kinderpostzegels—Stamps for the Children. Participating in this opened doors to neighbours and people within a couple blocks from where I lived. It also opened my mind to all kinds of different people in our neighbourhood. There was the group home for adults with mental challenges; retired seniors; people of different religious backgrounds; the foreign "guest" workers who came to the Netherlands to create a better life for themselves and their families. As a child, growing up quite protected, it made me realize there was another world out there.

My visit to one family stood out: a former "guest" worker opened the door, his wife alongside and several kids peeking around their parents. He said he did not have much money, but was it okay, could he give just a couple guilders? I said, yes, of course that was okay; I thanked him for his donation and told him I very much appreciated his donation.

And I did, because I learned that the most generous people have little or no money.

After coming to Canada in 1985 to take a position as a nanny in a northern Alberta community, I did more canvassing for the usual charity organizations. The most amazing experiences were going on volunteer work trips with Kindness in Action. They are a dental care group started by Albertan, Amil Shapka, that serves low-income groups in urban Alberta and now reaches out to remote places in the world, such as a makeshift clinic in Honduras.

In 2015, I had the opportunity to go with Kindness in Action to China, and in 2017, to Otuzco in Peru. The rural populations we visited were so thankful for the care they received. People would travel from remote farms and neighbouring villages and wait patiently. They would arrive in the morning and stay around for up to six hours, waiting patiently to get help to have their mouths checked, cleaned and teeth filled or pulled. Beautiful people, wind-burned, dressed in their best clothing, sat in the shade of a barn visiting, while the chickens, pigs and dogs would wander about. The locals who organized the event made good with what equipment was available. Boards, doors on sawhorses, school benches pushed together to make tables for patients to lay on.

Eating the local foods, sleeping in a dorm with our wool sweaters and toques on because it was so cold at night was an incredible opportunity for introspection. Seeing how hard the women worked, tending to all the livestock, milking yaks, cultivating vegetable gardens, taking care of their families and feeding three warm meals to all of us volunteers was humbling and inspirational.

People with so little, yet so happy and appreciative. The farmer, with only a couple teeth left, which needed to be pulled because they were infected and hurting, giving us a thumbs up the next morning because the pain was gone.

Some just wanting to hold your hand for comfort as the triage nurse or dentist checked what treatment was needed. Such a simple but oh-so-human gesture to feel connected to another caring human. To receive a big hug and a *gracias* from a complete stranger, free of dental pain after long suffering, was a touching reward.

One certainly does not have to go on world trips to help those in need. There are many seniors, veterans old and young, people with disabilities alone or with a caregiver, families, single parents, First Nations, Métis, Inuit, immigrants, working poor, addicts, alcoholics, couples in crisis and many lonely single persons who live in difficult circumstances and conditions within our communities.

For the last five years, I have been involved with our local food bank. A great team of volunteers ensures that these fellow Canadians and community members receive hampers to lighten their burden a little. These volunteers work hard and try to do so with an open mind and without judgement and with caring and consideration, empathy and understanding for their fellow human beings. And these fellow human beings are so grateful and appreciative of what is done to help them. Here, too, we receive the occasional hug (before Covid, and I hope, again, after Covid), and even a Christmas card wishing us a Merry Christmas and a Happy New Year, thanking us for what we do. I ask you, what MORE could you wish for?

We are so lucky that we have so many services available in Canada. Even now, with COVID-19 creating sickness and death and havoc around the world. Right now, those of us in the Western world get a taste of what it is like to do without, make do with what we have. Appreciate our food and toilet paper supplies AND suppliers, our health, our healthcare workers, our healthcare system, as well as living in a generally safe and very affluent country.

MY ADVICE...

Volunteering makes you feel good. You are making a difference in the life of a fellow human being. You grow as a person, and it keeps you grounded.

WORDS TO LIVE BY

"I raise up my voice—not so I can shout but so that those without a voice can be heard....We cannot succeed when half of us are held back."

–Malala Yousafzai, Pakistani activist for female education and the youngest Nobel Prize laureate

THE EMPTY NICHE

Susa Silvermarie

Susa Silvermarie is a widely published and anthologized poet who is grateful to spend her third trimester of life in Ajijic, Mexico. Her latest collection, available on Amazon, is *Poems for Flourishing*. She blogs at: www.susasilvermarie.com

The statue had been missing a long time. But I could feel it there the way the absence of a loved one can sometimes feel like presence. The niche was high on the outside of the church that I passed every day in Lecce, Italy. Some said the niche was never filled, that the church lost its patron funding back in the late 1500s, and the elegant facade was left incomplete. Others said the statue had been stolen sometime during the centuries it functioned as a parish church.

Me, I think the statue is there, under an invisibility spell. In fact, I perceive the missing statue to be the being most likely to succeed under an invisibility spell, an old woman. Here's the thing, the old woman in the empty niche talks to me sometimes. So, I've taken to asking her advice as I pass by.

Yesterday, I found a quiet corner across the street from the church. Leaning on a pillar of Lecce's partially excavated Roman Amphitheatre, I gazed over at the empty niche and lit up a cigarette. Pretending sophistication while I was actually petitioning an invisible statue for assistance. But you know how it is when you're a mess, but you don't even know what your problem is? It was like that. I was too muddled for my request to be specific.

It didn't matter. The Lady of the Empty Niche was the kind of listener we all wish for. She inclined her ear with perfect patience and let me sputter and sigh my way along. By the time I lit up my second cig, I was getting a bit more clear, silently telling her how lonely I felt, how touch-deprived and isolated. Admitting this to an invisible statue was weirdly consoling. Especially since, in my work as a counselor, I regularly reassured clients that we were all connected—in the Quantum Field, or Indira's Net, or in whatever divinity the client professed. Well, reassured everyone but me, evidently.

The Lady's compassionate silence was so filled up with attentiveness that I had to brush away tears. I stopped my inner stammering and stared with unfocused vision at the whole niche. Her listening aura gave me a clear sense of her shape. The Lady's gentleness was in her posture, an ageless Madonna leaning forward to hear me. To hear. Me!

Brushing away more tears, I apologized to the Lady that I didn't have any frankincense or myrrh. No sweetgrass or copal, not even sage. I said goodbye and, with an unobtrusive bow of thanks, blew her a perfect smoke ring. The offering of tobacco sailed across the street, and, I swear on my Italian grandmother's head, ascended in baroque grace right up to her empty niche. Ah, acknowledged. Isn't that all we really want?

A FAVOURITE QUOTE...

"Collective awakening is the hope of our planet. And collective awakening is possible."

–Thich Nhat Hanh

FOR MY YOUNGER SELF...

Dear younger self, if you could only see

how I've become your progeny.

Little Ancestor, look,

your trust in fun has bloomed in me.

Your belief in magic grew

to be a beanstalk to my dreams.

Younger one, oh listen.

I sing as unafraid as you

when you climbed the backyard maple tree

to belt out Davy Crockett.

As your descendant, so to speak,

I want to reassure you that

your aloneness in the crowded family

blossomed into poetry and joy.

So younger self, I send no counsel

back to where you sing

hidden in the branches of the tree.

But only thanks, for staying true,

so I could come to be.

OUT OF THE MOUTHS OF BABES!

Bonnie Kachur

A retired teacher who enjoyed thirty years of teaching young children, Bonnie Kachur, spends her time with her husband and family, including nine grandchildren. Since Covid-19, her traveling, spending time in Palm Springs and book club get-togethers have been put on hold, but her days are still filled with spending time at the lake with family, playing piano, golfing and learning to play mahjong.

I grew up with five brothers in an active traditional home. My dad was the breadwinner, and my mom stayed home and kept our house in tip-top shape. She was my role model. Fast forward twenty-five years. My husband and I are working while raising three active boys in a lived-in house! I get a call from my mom saying she and dad are in town and will be over shortly. I say to our boys, "Quick, grandma is coming over. We have to tidy the house."

My youngest replies, "Why can't grandma see how we really live?"

Touché!

ADVICE TO MY YOUNGER SELF...

Get involved! Don't be afraid to make mistakes while trying new things because that's how you learn and build your confidence.

A SPECIAL MOMENT IN VENICE
Violet St. Clair

Violet St. Clair feels fortunate to be both mother and teacher, and to have traveled to over fifty countries. She has said that blessed doesn't even begin to describe her feelings.

Souvenirs are funny things: sometimes grand, sometimes simple, but always stirring and transporting. This year they have an added poignancy and magic. Slippers from India, Maasai jewelry, the blue eye of Turkey. Each one tells a story that tugs at the heartstrings.

Tonight, I am gazing at the Medusa mask on the wall, snakes stretching outwards.

My mother called it the "ugly one," but to me she mists my eyes and takes me back to Venice.

I was traveling with my son. As a child, he had always wanted to visit Venice. It had been a long train ride. We were both beat; it was near midnight. Gathering up our bits of luggage, we headed out of the station.

Venice didn't disappoint. It shimmered with light and glistened with water. We were mesmerized. People gathered by the waters of the Grand Canal, a shambolic brouhaha of tourists, pigeons, hawkers, ancient buildings and bridges. Our fatigue disappeared, and we found a spot where we dropped everything and sat. I bought two cups of wine from a colourful, grizzled man, and we toasted our first night in the City of Water.

A young man drifted by, fresh off the train. He sat down a few metres from us. Backpack, jeans and a battered guitar. While we watched, he settled it within his arms and began to play a popular U2 song. People stopped, joined in; cigarettes were passed; drinks were enjoyed; and the summer warmth relaxed us all.

My son and I enjoyed a companionable moment, not always possible with a sixteen-year-old, in the city of his dreams. No, she is not the ugly one. Now that my son has made Vancouver his home, she is the great comforter. A souvenir of a loving moment between a mother and her son.

FOR MY YOUNGER SELF...

If I could go back and hold the hand of myself...

I would say trust yourself and the process. It will work out.

Remember, a little prayer, a little gratitude and a little faith in yourself. Be kind.

Step by step, the centre will hold, and you will be just fine.

SAVED BY A FISH

Kathy Klaus

"Life is not measured by the number of breaths we take,

but by the moments that take our breath away."

–Vicki Corona, Maya Angelou, et al

In 2003, I was a wife, mother and small business owner of a rapidly growing company with international tentacles. I had inventory issues, employee concerns, impatient bankers and stress bursting from the seams.

On a lark, I joined a women's salmon fishing derby and invited three girlfriends to come and have some fun. None of us had fishing experience, but there was a costume party attached to the weekend, and it sounded like a great all-girls weekend.

When my line went "zing," we were all totally shocked. The adrenalin surge was one that I had never experienced. When "my monster from the depths" was netted, we were gobsmacked! It weighed in at 31.5 pounds, the derby winner!

My reaction was pure amazement. I couldn't believe the miracle of how, in a deep and wide ocean, such a large fish chose and found my one little hook. I hadn't sacrificed, worked for or earned the fish in any way. It felt like the universe had smiled and handed me a precious gift.

The life-changing aha! moment came that evening when I walked into the pub at the lodge and ladies, guides—well, everyone— stood, clapped and cheered. I was so surprised and touched that the thought that went through my head was, *I'm not getting enough clapping in my life.*

I realized that I had been busy *doing*...working hard and wearing myself out for less than the moment of joy that *being*, and one big fish, brought me.

I resolved at that moment to bring more passion, fun and laughter into my life. I realized that sheer effort and hard work could not guarantee the satisfaction that my heart needed. Within two years, because of the miracle of one big fish and the insight gained at that derby, I had sold my company and forged a new direction.

ADVICE TO MY YOUNGER SELF...

Gratitude is KING.

It's an attitude, a decision and a way of living that has immeasurable value.

Start everyday and retire every evening in thankfulness.

PERFECTLY "CROCKED"
Diane Epp

An elementary school educator for thirty years, Dianne Epp is retired and pursuing her passions: golf and book club. Her treasures are her husband of 38 years, their two children and four grandchildren. She is outwardly grateful for every day that is given her.

Note: like many families who create their own colloquialisms, "crocked" is the Epp's word for crooked.

My husband and I were hanging a large picture over our bed. Lloyd had to balance himself on the bed with his hammer and picture hooks. He is very particular about everything being level and straight.

With my help, we hung the picture. To me it looked PERFECT. Lloyd stepped back and asked me what I thought. I said, "Perfect."

He said, "It's crocked." He adjusted one corner and asked me again.

I told him it was perfect.

He said, "Crocked." Once again, he adjusted another corner of the picture. Again, he wanted to know how it looked. I told him once again that it was perfect.

By then I was rolling my eyes and thinking this was crazy. I couldn't see anything wrong with the level of the picture. He said he gave up. He couldn't get the picture hanging any better. I told him that it was perfect the first time.

"Oh," he said. "I thought you kept saying it was crocked."

MY ONE PIECE OF ADVICE...

Eat healthily, stay active, find joy in your family and friends. Make time for yourself.

Oh Canada!
Virginia Brown

Virginia Brown takes a great amount of pride in her community, a small town in central British Columbia. Her nursing career took her to long-term care, home care, a hospital and physicians' offices. For thirty-eight years, she has made it a pleasure to guide and teach young people in Air Cadets. Now retired, she volunteers with the RCMP in their Citizens On Patrol and Speed Watch programs.

I was born in South Africa and joined a large family of girls. Since my parents were absent, I was raised and educated in a Children's Home. It was a good place, and they looked after us very well, but I missed being part of my family.

My husband and I immigrated to Canada in the 1970s. The first unexpected event was when we landed in Toronto and walked out onto the airport grounds. It was the first time our youngest son had seen snow. He blurted out, "Look at all the sugar." People around us burst out laughing.

My first job as a registered nurse in Canada was working in an extended care facility. I spoke English so didn't realize that my

Afrikaans accent would pose a problem. Apparently, my accent was stronger than I thought as none of the patients could understand me. As time went on, I guess we all made adjustments, because they understand me just fine now.

I have lived in Canada for many years and still find myself teasingly explaining, "I don't speak with an accent...you listen with an accent."

MY ONE PIECE OF ADVICE...

Love your family and enjoy every moment that you spend with them.

Always be honest and truthful. Work hard and follow your dreams.

WORDS TO LIVE BY

"My mother told me to be a lady. And for her, that meant be your own person, be independent."

–Ruth Bader Ginsberg, second female justice
appointed to the U.S. Supreme Court

Surrounded by Story Retreat
Breakout Room Three

Welcome back. Readjust and get comfortable. If there was something you thought you wanted to have with you, then decided it was too much trouble—a fresh teabag, a snack plate, a shower and your robe—reconsider and take the time to treat yourself.

We Are All Artists…

For generations, women have told their stories through art. Their handicrafts are original, each a masterpiece whether beaded, quilted or embroidered. There's more. Things you do that you might not think are art.

Art speaks of its creator, shares about the environment and becomes a history book. Take birchbark biting, a traditional Cree art. An Indigenous woman will carefully separate thin pieces of bark, folding it many times, then placing it between her teeth. At that time, she will visualize an image then bite on the bark, turning the piece to represent or recreate the image in her mind.

Other artists bake bread—first at their grandmothers' sides then alone, and later—if they are fortunate—with a young person beside them. The stories are told during the rise and when the bread is broken. Is this not art? From scrapbooking to cross-stitch, our movements and words create art. And all art communicates story and connects people. The written word is a powerful, expressive art form. You are an artist.

Stop. Read that last part again. I'll say it for you: You are an artist. The act of putting pen to these pages makes it so.

In effect, you are a work of art.

You are an artist and a work of art because you are story and storyteller.

Note the repeat of "art" in the word heart.

YOU ARE AN ARTIST

Think not? Here's a challenge. Take anything you do and observe your unique style. There's rhythm in putting on the kettle, and you might have been humming, too. There is movement in making the bed; look at those sheets billow. There's a hop in your step, a pattern in your drive to work, a story in your tears. You are an artist in a retreat. This retreat. I know, isn't that incredible? Yes, you are.

What are all the unique ways you are an artist? What are your favourite ways to convey messages? It's okay, you don't have to have all the answers.

What other art forms would you like to explore?

Choose a specific positive memory connected to your artfulness:

What are your ideas for keeping that memory fresh and vivid?

Return to one, or all, of the photos of the Storytellers. Based only on visual, which one would you most like to meet? Describe her.

Example: Contributor, Janice Kimball is a multi-creative weaver and writer. Enjoy a tour of her gallery in Mexico https://mexicoandbeyond2016.blog/2019/11/19/penthouse-gallery.

An Unforgettable Year

The Covid Days of 2020 and 2021 provided multiple challenges, and no doubt, we have all done our best. This story recounts some of my reaction on our return to Canada from our winter season in Puerto Vallarta.

Given that we are mostly self-isolating and not dressing up to go anywhere, I have become rather slovenly in my personal habits. Here it is August, and I still have my Snowbird suitcases from Puerto Vallarta that are only partially unpacked. In my bathroom, my vanity is carelessly crowded with care products: cleanser, moisturizer, rub-on hormones...you know the drill. Yesterday morning I grabbed a familiar shape, as I have been doing over these past months and applied my underarm deodorant. I put my glasses on and, for the first time in months, looked at the label and discovered that I have been applying sunscreen to my underarms since April. Really? A mammoth cosmetic company has to reuse the packaging that everyone recognizes as deodorant?

My initial reaction to Covid vacillated between annoyance and a lazy kind of "Oh, well" acceptance. As the months went on to reveal the horror of sickness and death, the social isolation led to more snacking than EVER and, more seriously, a deep sadness. It took quite some time to adapt to the mindset of not travelling or visiting with family. Zoom calls became a norm, as did online memorials. The masks that completely obscured smiles and any sense of community represented desolation for me. As time passed, I developed profound gratitude for loved ones, my home, the freedom to rediscover many creative arts and appreciating a new way to connect with people. I also realized that all the extras weren't necessary after all…and my priorities had changed.

What has been your experience with Covid? Lessons learned?

How have you coped with the losses?

A FAVOURITE QUOTATION

"Well, I bought a ticket to the circus. I don't know why I was surprised to see elephants."

–Norris Church Mailer

Published in *The New Jersey Record/Herald News* on Nov. 23, 2010. North Jersey.com:

She was half the age of Norman Mailer when they met, and their bond was as fast and fateful as a mortal's coupling with a god. Norris Church Mailer, the Pulitzer Prize–winning author's sixth and final wife, would enjoy and endure the ride of her life.

An actress, Wilhelmina model, author and painter, Norris passed away after a long and valiant struggle with cancer at the age of 61. As Norris Mailer wrote in her 2010 memoir, *A Ticket to the Circus*, she was a single mother in her mid-20s when she met then-52-year-old Norman Mailer at a 1975 cocktail party in his honor in Russellville, Arkansas.

Their attraction was immediate, even if he was breaking up with his fourth wife and seeing the woman who would become his fifth. Norris Church became No. 6 in 1980.

The Norris Church Mailer quotation often pops into my mind when I reflect on the decisions I've made in my life. The quote reminds me that each and every choice has a consequence—one that, as I brood and muse, I MIGHT have seen coming.

How do you interpret Norris Church Mailer's quotation?

"Well, I bought a ticket to the circus. I don't know why I was surprised to see elephants."

Is there a quote that comes to mind when you are making decisions?

HUMOUR HELPS

Healthy humour can help us cope with the tough times in life. Laughing is an effective way to strengthen immune functions, bring more oxygen to the body and brain, foster positive feelings and improve interpersonal skills. Laughter Yoga Clubs have grown around the globe as it is understood that combining voluntary laughter with yogic breathing (pranayama), playful exercises and activities can promote well being.

What makes you laugh?

Certain words:

Situations:

Particular acts—stage, television, film:

Where does humour appear in your daily life?

SHENANIGANS

My husband and I traveled internationally for business frequently. When our sons were in their teens, their promises of being responsible and good stewards of our home during our absence deserved a prize in oratory. Upon our return, the housekeeping could not be faulted: dishes were done, vacuuming—even under the sofa, bathroom mirrors shone, the garage had been swept. Upon closer inspection, however, I noticed a peculiar stain on the carpet in my husband's closet, and the Norman Rockwell decorative plates on our display wall were hung grossly unevenly—perhaps by a drunken sailor. In retrospect, I'm sure the party signs went up on the highway before we boarded our flight. That only happened once … maybe!

Did you pull a few fast ones on your parents? Have you ever confessed or felt the need for full disclosure? Do these make for the best stories now? Write about the memory and immerse yourself in the joy of it.

Time Travel

If, similar to the Noah of Ark fame, you were packing for a trip that you may never even complete—perhaps wouldn't be unpacked for a hundred years, what would you put into your vessel? What are the things/symbols that represent you that you would want to include? Why?

The Power of Words

We think about our words as being clear because we know what we mean when we speak or write them. Unfortunately, their meaning isn't always perfectly understood by the listener, who is in his/her own head. Even when we do master the message, language evolves as the current generation adapts words to fit new meanings. Our constant use of electronic conversation doesn't allow us to see how our words land—in those cases, facial expression and body language do not contribute to the communication.

If you can think of a time when a funny situation or a conflict developed because of a misspoken word or misunderstood conversation, share it here.

A MOUNTAIN OF MISGIVINGS

When looking at a mountain, there are typically two ways of viewing it: one from the bottom and one from the top. Would you like to move toward something new but are plagued with excuses? Too much time…too little money…it's too hard.…It's silly to even think about it.

Instead of looking at the mountain and fearing if you could reach the top, would it help to imagine the new you at the top of the mountain, looking down to where you are now and what it would take to close the distance? Is your conundrum worth some reverse engineering? Or at least a diagram or a sentence or two:

ACT ONE

If you were to write a three-act play, and the working title was "My Life, Then and Now," what would be the central theme of the first act? Who will be the characters? Where is it set? Can you share at least two interactions that take place or recount a monologue, dialogue or excerpt of your choosing?

Rough notes:

Words I will use:

Bit of an outline:

Here I go:

ARE YOU CHARGED UP?

In this ever-changing, busy world, self care has never been more important.

What tools have you used in the past to recharge? Are they still working for you?

How do you relax?

In his book, *The Awe Factor*, famed author Allen Klein, suggests that a fifteen-minute walk in nature with the intention of finding "awe" can be healing—the structure and colour of a flower, the lacey pattern of the trees against the sky, the mossy footpath.

Visualize the most enjoyable times that you have spent outdoors. Take me with you on an Awe Factor walk.

Inspired by: Mr. Jollytologist, Allen Klein, MA,CSP
www.allenklein.com

A ROOM WITH YOUR VIEW

A ROOM WITH YOUR VIEW

4

LOVE REMEMBERED

KEYNOTE: LOVE REMEMBERED

Highlights

- Our loved ones want to be remembered

- Memories help us to grieve and heal

- Relationships can continue beyond death

What a pleasure to hear the stories of strong women through the voice of a family member. These stories help to adjust our perspective and bring meaning to the quote from Helen Keller: "What we have once enjoyed we can never lose; all that we deeply love becomes a part of us."

Regardless of how people show their love when they are here, they leave behind scrapbooks, photos and stories. Through the hooked rugs, hockey cards and recipe boxes stuffed with index cards and magazine clippings, our loved ones want to be remembered—and we want the ones who outlive us to remember us.

The initials in the cement on the new driveway, the carved heart on a tree, Grandpa's raspberry patch, each leave an indelible mark of connection. As we gather for the traditional Thanksgiving dinner and comment on the walnuts in Aunt May's special dressing and how Jimmy spilled the wine last year, we again enjoy the closeness of family. These are the moments that help us remember treasured, shared times. These are the memories that help us to grieve and heal.

In 1995, psychologist Louise J. Kaplan's book, *No Voice is Ever Wholly Lost* came forward with a landmark view of mourning. Kaplan explained that mourning is not about relinquishing our relationships with the deceased, but about finding appropriate ways to stay connected.

In Allison Gilbert' book *Passed and Present, Keeping Memories of Love Ones Alive,* she explores 85 memory-preserving ideas called Forget Me Nots. The entire collection serves as a reminder: keeping the memory of your loved one alive can be done easily, at any stage of the grieving journey, and that doing so can bring enormous pleasure.

While imagining the *Wild Ride* project for women, I was reminded of the strong women who have passed through my life. In recalling their stories, I realize that some of their values became my values and provided the connection and bedrock support for my journey. The following memory continues to warm my heart:

> My boyfriend, who later became my husband, and I took a twelve-hour bus ride across the prairies so that I could meet his parents for the first time.
>
> Upon arrival, we learned that a picnic was being held by the river and we travelled together, anticipating the fun and games. His mother and I were a team in an egg-catching contest, where we stood fifteen feet apart and tossed a raw egg between us, catching it in bare hands (a recipe for disaster!). When it was my turn, she leaned forward, and my throw hit her chest and the egg disappeared down the gap in her blouse. We all heard the splat, and while my reaction was open-mouthed shock, she fell to the ground laughing…and she laughed until tears ran down her face. That was the day I learned that laughter breaks down barriers, covers awkwardness and has a place in good, and seemingly disastrous, situations. She was the mother-in-law of my dreams!

> "Carve your name on hearts, not tombstones. A legacy is etched into the minds of others and the stories they share about you."
>
> –Shannon Alder

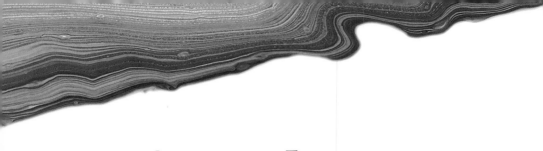

TEA, COOKIES AND FORTITUDE
Annie Cherwinski (1902–88)
Submitted by Antonia Gossner, granddaughter

Annie was born in 1902 in Austria and came to Canada at a young age with her mother and siblings. They joined her father on a homestead in Saskatchewan. At the age of seventeen, she was married to Anton Cherwinski. This marriage was arranged by the fathers of the couple and, though they had met only once before exchanging their vows, they lived and worked together in harmony for over 66 years, raising a son and two daughters and creating a family farming operation that still exists today.

My paternal grandmother, Annie, was a storyteller, a nurturer and an extremely intelligent woman who knew her own mind, spoke her own truth and never suffered fools gladly. Had she been born today, I have no doubt that she would have headed up some large and successful business and provided it with a unique style of leadership—affectionate, no-nonsense and practical.

I have always admired her, looked up to her and tried to become as much like her as I possibly can. For me, she was Mother and Home.

She also was known for her wry humour and dry wit. On one occasion, I remember her engaging in a conversation over tea and cookies with a number of her contemporaries—Slavic women in their sixties and seventies. It seemed that most of those in the group were concerned that when their time came, their descendants might not provide them with a funeral as elegant, decorous and proper as they would like.

My grandmother listened to the various complaints and concerns for a while, then spoke up firmly: "No…I'm not at all troubled! When my time comes, I will lay back, my eyes closed, my arms crossed, a prim little smile on my face and I will chuckle to myself, 'Not my problem anymore! I'm dead! Let someone else worry themselves sick about everything for a change!'"

Comment from Antonia:

This discussion was possible because my grandmother and her friends were no strangers to death, having attended deaths in their families and communities as young women, and because they were possessed of a strong faith in God and the afterlife. As a child who spent a great deal of time in her presence, I absorbed her straightforward belief and acceptance.

Later in my life, I was honoured to be present at her deathbed and, at various times, with other loved ones. And while, of course, I experienced grief and sorrow, I was neither afraid nor overwhelmed. My grandmother's gift to me was the knowledge that every life must come to an end, and that every end is, in fact, a wondrous new beginning.

MY ONE PIECE OF ADVICE…

God, family and prayer,

then work hard and do your duty…

Bonus Mom

Mary Jane Fontaine (1936–2018)
Submitted by Linda Gillen

Mary Jane Fontaine, "Janie," enjoyed her work at the University of Washington Art Department. She was a perpetual art student and especially enjoyed painting and sculpture. She was a queen in the kitchen, creatively pulling together a gourmet meal from leftovers in her refrigerator. Despite many challenges, she was lighthearted—a positive, happy spirit. Upon her passing, all the artists from her workplace designed incredible quilt squares for a fabric art quilt that became a treasure that brought warm and happy memories.

I met my Bonus Mom after I had school-age children of my own. My father remarried after my mom passed, Janie became his devoted and loving partner. They had the loving kind of relationship that you sometimes see in older couples; sweet, adoring and always holding hands. They travelled widely in their motorhome, built a house together and shared several good years.

My relationship with Janie revolved around our common interests in gardening, going to the theatre, walking around the lake and the board games that she enjoyed playing. She loved to tell me stories of her earlier, very difficult marriages, but also about the good times in her life. Our connection blossomed into a very close mother-daughter friendship.

I especially admired her strength as my dad's dementia progressed. She was so tender and helpful to him; never rolling her eyes or showing impatience with his antics, as many might have done. I remember him offering me a glass of wine from the coffee pot in which he had poured a full bottle of wine. Janie remarked, "Oh, I think we'll just share that."

Janie and I became close friends as I watched her patiently, lovingly take care of my dad the last four years of his life, as he slowly slipped away mentally with Alzheimer's. She was a remarkable example of how love found late in life can be the sweetest of all.

MY ONE PIECE OF ADVICE...

Always look on the bright side.

WHISTLES OF LOVE

Anita Paulsen Holstein
Submitted by her daughter, Nila Nielsen

My mom, Anita Paulsen Holstein, was an inspiration to many. She was a country schoolteacher for 38 years and was remembered fondly by her students. Mom was creative. She would write plays, compose songs and create stage back-drops for the yearly community Christmas program. In her spare time, she was a farmer's wife, working alongside dad when needed, and she forever had something cooking for the neighbors to eat. Anita and the New Sounds was the name of her "hobby"—a four-piece band she started. They played Friday and Saturday nights. According to Mom, it was important to bring music to people to "help them forget all their troubles." Everyone in eastern Nebraska and western Iowa knew Anita and celebrated the joy she brought them. Every evening she would relax and unwind by playing the piano or organ—any song you named, she could play it by ear. She would take turns playing our favorite songs as we fell asleep. It was comforting to know that her love for us was felt deeply within those songs.

My mother, Anita, didn't share this story except once—on her deathbed. My siblings and I had two unforgettable days to share memories and laugh with her prior to her death.

During this time, we asked her if there was anything special she wanted us to know. She hesitated, but then smiled as she began to share what she said was a secret that she had kept since the first year of marriage to our dad. Her eyes brightened, and she chuckled when she added that she was only sharing it with us now because the love of her life, Elmer, had died many years before, and she knew he wouldn't mind.

She explained that during the first year of their marriage, as a young farm wife, she would miss Elmer when he was outside working.

One day, she heard three short, but loud whistles coming from the barn. She knew it was him, as he loved to whistle songs while he worked, but this was different. She feared something had happened. She ran quickly toward the barn where he was walking out laughing and asked, "Did you hear that?" When she nodded yes, he said, "Good, I was whistling I Love You."

From then on, when Mom heard those three wonderful whistles, she knew he was thinking about her.

As children, we each remembered hearing those whistles many times, but until that moment had never understood the true meaning behind those heartfelt whistles of love. It was their secret, and it meant the world to her, and now to us as well.

MOM'S ADVICE WOULD BE...

"Always keep a song in your heart and a smile on your face." She said it often and lived it daily.

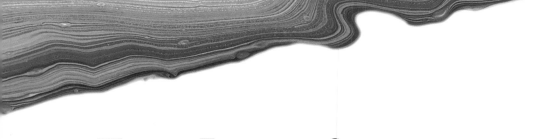

WEDDING THRILLS AND SPILLS

Mary Emily Love
Submitted by her daughter, Sharon Love Cook

Mary Emily Love was originally from Finland—her name was Meime Amilia Haapa-Koski, which translated into "American" as Mary Emily.

My mother was free with her advice. One common remark concerned my tendency to spill on myself. I'm afraid it still holds true today. Decades later, I can't help being a food magnet.

I remember buying a wedding dress in the early '70s. Back then, the hippie era, weddings were casual affairs; people got married barefoot, in jeans. The idea of buying a big white dress was unimaginable. Thus, I compromised, searching for a suit: a dress and jacket. Before I left the house, my mother warned, "Whatever you do, don't buy white. You know how you spill all over yourself."

Her words stung. "It's a bridal outfit." I pointed out. "What am I supposed to wear, paisley?"

"Anything but white," she said, always having the last word.

I deliberately bought white: an elegant, sleeveless, winter-wool dress with matching jacket. Naturally, my mother was appalled.

The wedding reception was held at a local country club. I was cautious as we sat down to eat. After the blessing and the toasts, dinner was served. My elderly aunt launched into a nostalgic story; I leaned across the table to hear. At some point I noticed my jacket lapel floating in the gravy boat. I removed it, causing gravy to trail down the front of my dress. This was not lost on my mother. I couldn't hear her words over the music, but I knew what she was saying: "I told you not to buy white!"

'Twas ever thus.

MY ONE PIECE OF ADVICE...

Never wear white (because you'll spill all over yourself).

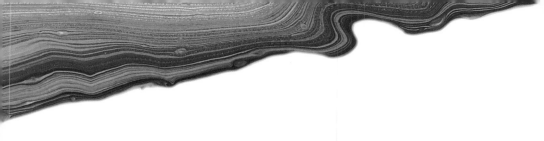

WHAT SIZE?

Lillian J. O'Brien
Submitted by her daughter, Patti Heerhartz

Lillian J. O'Brien and her
husband, a military officer, had
three daughters. She had many
friends, was artistic, a good
Catholic and she loved the role of
being a colonel's wife.

During World War II, my dad was stationed overseas. He sent my
mom regular letters, often included a list of things he needed for
her to send in the mail. She religiously took these lists to the Air
Force Base Exchange (store) to purchase the items he requested.

One such list included a jock strap. Obviously, Mom had NO
idea what this was. But she took his list, and a male employee
asked if he could help her. When she mentioned the jock strap,
the employee asked her, "What size?"

She looked him over and said, "He's about the same size as you
are."

My godmother told me this story—my mom would have never admitted it—and to this day, whenever I think of it, I still laugh until tears roll down my face.

WORDS TO LIVE BY

"I'd rather regret the things I've done than regret the things I haven't done."

–Lucille Ball, Actor

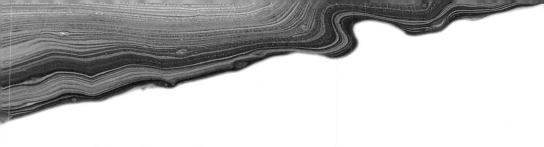

THE PINK DRESS

Martina Massett Schnell
Submitted by her granddaughter, Kathy Tipman

Born in Strasburg, Russia, in 1892, Martina immigrated to Canada with her family. She and her sister married two brothers, hence they had the same maiden and married names. My Great Aunt Katherine died at the age of 22, six months after giving birth to her third child—a loss for many, including her sister, Martina.

As a child, I visited my grandmother, Martina Masset Schnell, on her farm every summer vacation. I relished those weeks of freedom to roam and the undivided personal attention from my grandmother. I spent hours questioning her about her childhood as part of a German colony on the Russian Steppes in the late 1800s. Many stories were of her life there, but she also had stories about her family's emigration to Canada. These were all fascinating stories to me as I had never been more than fifty miles from my place of birth.

My last meaningful visit with my grandmother was during my early twenties when I was very keen on genealogy. During our conversation, I took notes of a few of her stories. She also gave me a picture of her and her sister, Katherine. The following is a direct quote from this interview.

"I remember being on the train in England and seeing laundry hung out on a clothesline. Amongst the clothes was a pretty, pink dress that looked to be about my size. I was ten at the time, and I thought that dress was the most beautiful thing I had ever seen. My parents had talked about all of the land they would have in Canada and that they would work hard and soon have a lot of money. How I hoped that would mean I could have a pink dress like the one I saw. Life did not work out that way. My family never had any money, and I never had a pink dress. I just had a lot of children, and I had to work hard all of my life."

Years later, I found myself on a train from England's Gatwick Airport to central London, speeding through some poorer neighbourhoods. Several of the houses had laundry hanging out on clotheslines, and I was reminded of my grandmother's story. Yes, Martina did have a hard life on the Canadian prairies, and she gave birth to fourteen children, eleven of whom lived to be adults. She never had many fine material possessions like pink dresses, but I wondered if that was an accurate measure of her life's value. Martina is survived by over two hundred direct descendants, many of whom, like me, relish our memories of this quiet and loving woman, and are very appreciative of her journey and the life she helped to build for us in Canada. Thank you, Grandma.

GRANDMA'S ADVICE...

If my grandmother, a very devout Catholic, was to give her future descendants any advice, I am sure it would be to follow the teachings of the church. Her emphasis would be on being a good wife and mother and taking good care of our families. Few of us are still practicing Catholics, but most of us have done our best by our families.

GRANDMA AND ME

Marion Armstrong Leach
Submitted by her granddaughter, Diane Dique

Life was hard during the depression. My grandma, Marion Armstrong Leach, remained a strong force throughout. Through the many stories she shared, I learned the importance and value of family.

First off, let me say, I miss my Grandma, and I'm almost 70 years old! I only ever knew one grandma, and she always lived close enough that I could walk to her home—and I did, many, many times. Especially when I was on the outs with my mom, her only daughter. Grandma was widowed in her thirties.

I have many stories of my time with her, sleepovers in her bed, with the chamber pot underneath. My hair curled in rags for church the next morning, bricks of Neapolitan ice cream cut into four. A slab for each of my two bachelor uncles and one each for Grandma and me.

She had a wonderful sense of humour. As a youngster, I remember one night, during a sleepover in her bed, she whispered that I wasn't to worry about the open window. "If the boogeyman ever came, he'd take one look at me without my teeth and jump right back out! So, you have nothing to be afraid of." She'd end that with a hug and kiss on the cheek. Grandma always made me feel special and loved. It's pretty wonderful when you're a kid that seems to find trouble!

About three months before I was to be married, Grandma and I were enjoying a leisurely afternoon visit over tea and biscuits. I was talking about marriage and wondering what it would be like. Would I really be happy? Was this what I wanted? Could I measure up—be the good wife? Would I have to change who I was? My mother-in-law to be could cook and bake and sew and garden, she even went back to college in the '70s against her husband's wishes. She could pretty much do anything!

My grandmother listened to my worries and then told me how there were times in her marriage that she'd thought about leaving, but decided to stay because, "Where would I go?" She had married young, losing her first child at age four to meningitis. She'd had three more children, a daughter and twin sons with special needs. Grandma was from a strong family and told me their strength helped her through many hard times, especially when my grandfather died at 35 years of age. She found great strength in her faith. It didn't bother her that others in her family weren't as committed. As we talked, Grandma said it was important to laugh with your husband and do things together no matter how busy you were. And make sure I looked after myself. I should be sure to challenge my husband to be a better partner and not do everything for him. "He needs to appreciate you."

"If you're making him bacon and eggs for breakfast, you should break the yolks every once in awhile." Those words have become the words to live by that I've never forgotten!

When our children were born, she told me many times that, "you're an instant millionaire when you are blessed with a child." I have never forgotten that. She was a kind grandma but took no nonsense. I cherish her memory and thank her for instilling in me what is important in this life.

GOOD ADVICE...

Practice the Golden Rule:

Do unto others as you would have done to you.

We all make mistakes. Just remember to say you're sorry and mean it.

I LOVE YOU

Joan Canal Schoeffel
Submitted by her daughter, Alicia Robinson

A spiritual woman, Joan loved her family deeply. A nurse, then nursing instructor, she eventually earned a PhD in educational psychology and worked primarily to help young people in areas of nutrition and teen pregnancy prevention. She also wrote award-winning grants. Joan was an awesome woman— compassionate, intelligent, caring, creative, funny. Her family meant everything to her. She loved babies and treasured her own children and her seven grandchildren. She particularly adored the opera, and the Florida sunshine and beaches.

Joan Schoeffel's actions spoke louder than her words.

She walked the walk. Losing her husband to cancer when he was only 33 and left with three young children, she raised them on her own. There were some hard times, times when the electric bill didn't get paid, but the children always had their needs met, especially their need for a mother's overflowing love. All three children earned college degrees and are happily married, two with children of their own. As her bio notes, Joan went back to

217

school as her children got older, earning a PhD in educational psychology.

In addition to her life example, she shared sayings that helped my perspective and contributed to my positivity:

"You catch more flies with honey than you do with vinegar.

"A broken clock is right twice a day."

"How do you eat an elephant? One bite at a time."

"Aren't the strawberries beautiful?" She said that this was what a man said as he was falling off a cliff, to his death, as he noticed strawberries growing out of the side of the cliff.

She later gave me a strawberry printed nightgown, and over the years, I gave her gifts with strawberries, too.

When I was eighteen and ready to run away from home, she said something I've never forgotten. As I stood in the living room crying, she said, "We're all scared. We all don't know what to do at times." These words changed my life. I thought everyone was confident and knew what to do. I realized I was not alone and that being eighteen didn't mean I had to know it all. Neither does anyone have to know it all at sixty-one.

This past year, on February 3rd, Joan passed at age eight-two after a long experience with Alzheimer's disease. I hesitate to say a battle because, despite the ravages of the disease, she bore them with grace and dignity. To the end, she looked good. She kept her kindness intact, and for that reason, she was a favourite of caregivers. There never seemed to be a time without a smile and laugh, a twinkle in her eye. Even with the disease, I felt like she knew who I was—at times—by the way she looked at me, touched my hair or held my hand.

In the last several weeks of her life, she was mostly sedated and did not speak much. But, on the last visit I had with her, when she was able to speak and breathe normally, she took my hand, looked me in the eyes with great clarity—the Alzheimer's seemed to be gone, briefly—and said, "I love you." There are no more important or meaningful words.

ADVICE TO MY YOUNGER SELF OR OTHERS...

A broken clock is right twice a day.

WORDS TO LIVE BY

"A smile starts on the lips, a grin spreads to the eyes, a chuckle comes from the belly; but a good laugh bursts forth from the soul, overflows, and bubbles all around."

–Carolyn Birmingham

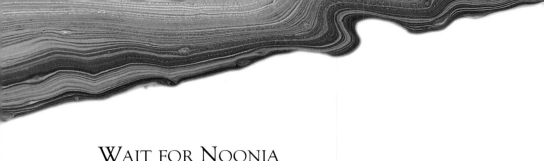

WAIT FOR NOONIA
Carrie Lenzen (1923-2003)
Submitted by her daughter, Antonia Gossner

Carrie Lenzen was born in 1923 to a homesteading family in Saskatchewan. It was hard to build a home and eke out a living on the Saskatchewan prairie in the 1920s. Life was hard, luxuries nonexistent, even necessities scarce. She married and raised four children, with few conveniences, on a busy farm. She is remembered by her extended family for her hospitality and making delicious pies. After the illness and death of her first husband, she remarried in 1983. Together they spent winters in Arizona, and Carrie was able to truly explore her talents in writing poetry, painting and crafting

When Carrie was five years old and her sister, Annie, was seven, they were often tasked the care of their three-year-old sister, Nastunia (who called herself Noonia). The older two tired of always having Nastunia around, putting a damper on their big kid games, and one day, they saw an opportunity and away they ran. Nastunia realized what was happening and gave chase, crying and begging, "Carrie! Annie! Please wait for Noonia!" But they kept running, eventually hiding in bushes, watching Nastunia's little legs tire, as she turned, sobbing and heartbroken, to return to their shack. Then they continued their play, free from their pesky little sister.

Days afterwards, scarlet fever struck the community. Carrie's family all became deathly ill, but eventually began to recover. Except for Nastunia. She was the baby, younger and weaker than the rest. Nastunia died. The family laid their baby to rest; the struggle for survival continued. But Carrie was consumed with grief, and her child's mind came to a terrible conclusion. It was all her fault! Nastunia had died because Carrie had been mean to her that day.

As she matured, Carrie's mind came to recognize the fallacy of that belief. Nevertheless, the incident haunted her for the rest of her life. She often retold the story to her children and grand-children and, shortly before her death, she confided that she still sometimes woke from a dream in which she, as a child, ran and ran and ran, pursued by a piercing wail: "Carrie, Carrie! Please wait for Noonia!"

Note from Antonia:

Those days are gone. In today's society, we have the necessities to survive, and still have time and energy to acknowledge that wounds happen to the mind and soul. We are developing skills for treatment and healing, and while it is unlikely every emotional trauma suffered by a child is recognized and treated, I know that many are.

And for that, Carrie would be very grateful.

MY ONE PIECE OF ADVICE...

Take care of yourself; you cannot pour from an empty vessel.

LEADING WITH HUMOUR

Millie Williams
Submitted by her son, Jim-Bob Williams

Millie was the first person I knew who practiced therapeutic humor. She was inspired by, and a great fan of, Erma Bombeck.

Millie Williams, born in Poland, was a manicurist in Brooklyn. She would make up outrageous stories just to see the reaction of her customers. For example, she referred to my dad as her third husband. They had civil, Jewish and Methodist services to satisfy the government and both sides of the family.

The customers would ask what kind of guy #3 was. She would tell them, "He's just so good with my kids." When a customer's Aunt Sadie was shot, my mom asked how things were going. The customer said, "The bullet is in her yet." My mom asked, "Tell me one thing, just where is Sadie's yet?" The woman almost passed out laughing.

At her cemetery, it was hard to think of her as gone. I remember looking out at the nearby plots. One was for the WISEMAN family, and one was for the GLASS family. Really big plaques marked the plots. My view was interrupted by a guy who was not one of her favorites. But the way he was positioned, blocking some of my line of sight, the plaques read WISE ASS. I burst out laughing, feeling sure she had arranged it.

FAVOURITE QUOTES FROM ERMA BOMBECK

"I come from a family where gravy is considered a beverage."

"When I stand before God at the end of my life, I would hope that I would not have a single bit of talent left, and could say, 'I used everything you gave me.'"

"Never go to a doctor whose office plants have died."

"If you can't make it better, you can laugh at it."

"Marriage has no guarantees. If that's what you're looking for, go live with a car battery."

SURROUNDED BY STORY RETREAT
Breakout Room Four

So…how are you? Have you felt like a character in "The Book of You," and at the same time the author?

Are there insights generated from having the examples from many Storytellers? Is there a new beginning in you?

Has any of what you have read or written sparked something you know you will not be able to leave alone, let go, forget?

Do you have any new perspectives and ideas? Are you more aware of your positive stories and that, with effort, you can retain these memories to enjoy into the future?

When I started this project, I was reflecting on my parents' stories, having observed that, in their later years, many of their memories were less than positive. I wondered what steps I could take to make it more likely that, in the future, my own recollections would include happy times and humorous moments.

The following helped me to gain a new understanding about the power of stories. Perhaps they will be useful when you choose recall as a companion to make decisions, as a tool for connection and as a soothing ritual.

1. We truly are surrounded by story. If you want to connect or pass along beliefs or family values, fold them into a story for maximum effect.

2. Strong emotions make memory better. It is suggested that the details in stories with powerful emotions like the element of surprise, fear, anger, betrayal may be remembered more easily.

3. To more readily remember positive memories, be truly aware in the moments of your life and be attentive to details. Occasionally recall the

imagery of the situation, engage the senses and practice bringing it back to your awareness.

4. Gratitude is associated with happiness and helps us to recall happy times with more detail. Gratitude rituals promote well-being. Expressions of thankfulness are a tonic for the world.

As you continue on your journey, the positive memories that you commit to retaining will warm your heart.

WHERE IS MY FOCUS?

Here are some criteria for creating a Mission Statement.

What you are doing,

How you are doing it,

Why you are doing it.

How would defining a focus be beneficial to you in the future?

Which of your values and beliefs are non-negotiable?

What are the central thoughts that you could consider in beginning to write a personal mission statement?

Examples of mission statements:

"To use my gifts of intelligence, charisma and serial optimism to cultivate the self-worth and net worth of women around the world."

–Amanda Steinberg, Dailyworth.com

"To serve as a leader, live a balanced life and apply ethical principles to make a significant difference."

–Denise Morrison, Former CEO of Campbell Soup Company

Not merely to survive, but to thrive; and to do so with some passion, some compassion, some humour and some style."

–Maya Angelou

HOPES AND DREAMS

The opposite of retreat is advance. As you go forward, will you be fully aware that you are an artist, that the creativity in you is infinite, that your heart cries out for expression.

What are the words and behaviours that will remind me that I am an artist?

Would you consider writing more in this or another journal, even gluing pictures in it or folding some of the pages? If so, what would be the first thing you'd stick in it and where? Tell yourself more about what filling this book could do for you:

Might you compose a gratitude letter or two? If so, do you have someone or someones in mind? Are they listed in the gratitude section, or have you since come up with more?

And the Ride Continues

Do you have superpowers that will help you to reach your goals? Are you a good listener, an excellent bread maker, a patient parent, a determined student, an organized teacher, an outspoken advocate, a caring home visitor, an expressive writer, a whizz at creating newspaper hats? We all have unique superpowers that help us navigate our lives. Often they are revealed in the tasks that we feel good about, the compliments that we receive and the niggling at the edge of our dreams.

Identify the top five superpowers that will enliven the journey as you continue on your wild ride.

Which would you like to explore and define in writing?

THE ONE YOU FEED

The Story of Two Wolves, a story offered by elders, (source anonymous).

An old Cherokee is teaching his grandson about life. "A fight is going on inside me," he said to the boy. One is evil; he is anger, evil, sorrow, regret, greed, arrogance, self-pity, guilt, resentment, inferiority, lies, false pride, superiority and ego."

The boy's eyes widened.

The elder continued, "The other is good; he is joy, peace, love, hope, serenity, humility, kindness, benevolence, empathy, generosity, truth, compassion and faith."

The boy breathed a sigh of relief, having heard there was something good there.

"The same fight is going on inside you, child, and inside every other person, too."

The grandson thought for a minute, then asked his grandfather, "Which wolf will win, Grandfather?"

The old Cherokee simply replied, "The one you feed."

My common sense tells me this sage advice applies to our memories.

We can't totally exclude negative memories, but the ones you feed, the ones that you review and give emotion to, are the ones that surface and affect the way you move forward.

Wondering how to feed the positive? Bring them to mind and relive the scents, tastes, textures, lighting and sounds. Do it as often as you want, you can never over-feed the positive.

Each time you recall an event, you strengthen your memory. Even more helpful, record the memory or write it. Try that for one here:

IF A PHOTO IS WORTH A THOUSAND WORDS

If your local newspaper requested a favourite photo of you celebrating, would you have one for them?

Do you have a photo of yourself that shows your eyes sparkling with excitement, delight obvious on your face? That's the photo to display on your refrigerator! If a photo can be a story, what better way to communicate your joy to all.

Review the photos that show your smiling and happy face, make a collage and use them for inspiration in the coming days.

What were you thinking about?

What was the occasion?

Relive that happiness and write about the experience.

If you were to have a grand opening, a "You Launch," what would be the components of that celebration?

The Finale: On Your Way

My gratitude to you for challenging yourself.

Kudos for participating in his unique, interactive experience.

My wishes and hopes for all:

Remember, you are an artist. You are a work of art. Everything you do has rhythm. All movement is a project. All thoughts are creativity.

Feed your positive memories by colouring in the details so that you can recall and enjoy them into the future. Welcome the unexpected…that's where the best stories live.

When you move about and think and connect with others, welcome adventure into your life…and go beyond that: Be the adventure in your life.

Continue your Wild Ride with kindness and courage so that all your stories are infused with YOU, the authentic human whose story is her life.

> "Courage is the most important of all the virtues
>
> because without courage,
>
> you can't practice any other virtue consistently."
>
> –Maya Angelou

You have been so kind to allow me into your world, I'd love to hear from you at kathy.klaus@me.com. Watch for news about the theme for the next *Wild Ride* anthology at surroundedbystory.ca.

ACKNOWLEDGEMENTS

Esteemed Storytellers

I am ever-so-grateful to the 55 guest Storytellers who put their heart and soul into their stories, providing a wealth of situations for enjoyment and reflection. None of us would be surrounded by this story had it not been for your contributions, encouragement and patience. You kindly responded to my invitation to submit a personal story for the original project, then consented to evolving.

my deepest gratitude

a river of loving and laughing souls

Founders and facilitators of the Humor Academy,

The Association For Applied and Therapeutic Humor

such joy you deliver.

Mary Kay Morrison,

Nila Nielsen, Bev Eanes, Laurie Young and The Besties,

Kathy Laurenhue, Linda Gillen,

Brenda Elsagher, Deb Price, Marietta Miller

For all your expertise and support that kept me on task...

an excess of appreciation

imagination becomes you

Shelley Tincher Buonaiuto

your trust in my proposal,

and your willingness to allow *Wild Ride* to be a catalyst to conception,

has been pivotal to this adventure

I'm awed by your talent

and grateful for your permission

Before I completed this book project, thrilled to collect authentic stories from gifted Storytellers, there was expansion in my peripheral: the collection begged further curating; the stories— sages on pages—were restless between the covers and ached for a further purpose.

literal and literary breath

Through a chance meeting, I met editor, Marie Beswick-Arthur, and little did I know how we would excel at team brainstorming and reimagine a book of service to women. Our collaboration, built on the original concept, organically evolved into a worthbook we swore had a life of its own.

Marie, your attention to tone and feeling have resulted in the warmer, softer blanket around the shoulders, soft place to fall approach we were determined to provide. Thank you for your belief in the power of sisterhood and this Wild Ride project.

I am deeply grateful to Marina Michaelides of Dragon Hill Publishing for taking on this project and publishing it under the

Rise Press imprint. To Shane who found a place for my work to live and to Ashley, Faye and Tamara for shepherding it through to its natural conclusion.

happily forever after

Thank you to my entrepreneurial, ever inspiring and caring family.

My husband, Larry, and sons, Jeffrey, Daniel, and Graeme

have a long history of encouraging my dreams

and cheerleading through to the finish line.

They wisely pulled me back from the edge

of the Saskatoon berry and alpaca farming schemes—

You guys are the best.

You bring energy and enthusiasm to every challenge.

Our family is my reward on this,
our shared and miraculous journey.

Always love, and love always

Isla and Jackson,

you are loved,

you are precious,

you are the legacy

and that's another story...

FROM MY BOOKSHELF

Creating Delight, Kathy Laurenhue with Bron Roberts and Sharon Wall

Expect a Miracle, Dan Wakefield

Laugh Out Loud, Allia Zobel Nolan

Love, Henri, Henri J.M. Nouwen

Passed and Present: Keeping Memories of Loved Ones Alive., Allison Gilbert

Postcards From Canada, Writers Foundation Strathcona County

Ringling Remembered, Ron Severini

Spoon River Anthology, Edgar Lee Masters

StoryQuest, Laura Lentz

The Language of Humor, Alleen Pace Nilsen and Don L F. Nilsen

Using Humor to Maximize Living, Mary Kay Morrison

What's Worth Knowing, Wendy Lustbader

When I Am an Old Woman, I Shall Wear Purple, Sandra Martz

Who Will Cry When You Die?, Robin Sharma

Writing Works, Bolton, Field, and Thomson

Your Glasses Are on Top of Your Head, Brenda Elsagher

Your Meaning Legacy, Laura A. Roser

Your Meaning Legacy Workbook, Laura A. Roser

Gendry, Sebastien. Laughter Online University, www.laughteronlineuniversity.com.

Kateria, Dr. Madan. Laughter Yoga International, www.laughteryoga.org.

Stand Up for Student Well Being. www.suswb.ca

The Comedy Cures Foundation. www.comedycures.org

RESEARCH SOURCES

The Value of a Story

Birren, James E. & Kathryn Cochrane Book. *Telling the Stories of Life Through Guided Autobiography Groups*. Baltimore, MD: Johns , 2001.

Frude, Neil & Steve Killick. "Family Storytelling and the Attachment Relationship." *Psychodynamic Practice*, 17:4, 2011, pp. 441-455, doi: 10.1080/14753634.2011.609025.

Roser, Laura A. *Your Meaning Legacy*. Yonker, NY: Golden Legacy Press, 2018.

Tomasulo, D.J & J.O. Pawelski. "The Use of Stories to Promote Positive Interventions." Positive Psychology Center, University of Pennsylvania, Philadelphia, USA. Psychology Department, New Jersey City University, Jersey City, USA, doi: 10.4236/psych.2012.312A176.

Memory and Emotion

Asperholm, M., Högman, N. Rafi, J. & Herlitz, A. "What did you do yesterday? A meta-analysis of sex differences in episodic memory." *Psychological Bulletin*, 145(8), 2019, pp. 785–821, https://doi.org/10.1037/bul0000197

Chen, Chong, Taiki Takahashi & Si Yang. "Remembrance of Happy Things Past: Positive Autobiographical Memories Are Intrinsically Rewarding and Valuable, But Not in Depression." *Frontiers in Psychology* 2015, doi.org/10.3389/fpsyg.2015.00222.

Fujita, F., Diener, E., & Sandvik E. "Gender Differences in Negative Affect and Well-being: The Case for Emotional Intensity." *Journal of Personality and Social Psychology*, 61(3), October 1991, pp. 427-34; doi:10.1037//0022-3514.61.3.427

Hamann, S. "Cognitive and Neural Mechanisms of Emotional Memory." *Trends in Cognitive Sciences*, Volume 5, Issue 9, 2001, pp. 394-400, doi.org/10.1016/S1364-6613(00)01707-1.

Kensinger, Elizabeth A. "How Emotion Affects Older Adults' Memories for Event Details." *Memory*, 17:2, pp. 208-219, doi: 10.1080/09658210802221425.

LeDoux, Joseph E. T*he Emotional Brain: The mysterious underpinnings of emotional life.* New York: Simon & Schuster, 1998

Selina. "Why Can't I Remember the Good Times." moonwalkingtojoy.com, February 26, 2021.

Speer, Megan E., Jamil P. Bhanji, & Mauricio R. Delgado. "Savoring the Past: Positive Memories Evoke Value Representations in the Striatum." Newark, NJ: Department of Psychology, Rutgers University, Open Archive Published October 30, 2014, doi.org/10.1016/j.neuron.2014.09.028

Tarrier, Nicholas. "Broad Minded Affective Coping (BMAC): A 'Positive' CBT Approach to Facilitating Positive Emotions." *International Journal of Cognitive Therapy.* Vol. 3, No. 1. March 2010, doi.org/10.1521/ijct.2010.3.1.64.

Young, Karen. "How to Feel Happier—According to Science. Using Positive Memories to Increase Positive Emotions." https://www.heysigmund.com › how-to-feel-happier.

Gratitude

Brown, Joshua, Joel Wong. "How Gratitude Changes You and Your Brain." *Greater Good Magazine*, June 2017 https://greatergood.berkeley.edu/

Emmons, Robert A. & Robin Stern. "Gratitude as a Psychotherapeutic Intervention." June 17, 2013, doi.org/10.1002/jclp.22020.

Heid, Markham. "The Power of Positive Memories: Remembering Happy Times May Offer Protection for Mental Health." December 5, 2019, elemental.medium.com/the-nuance/home.

The Launch Project. "5 Ways to Keep Happy Memories from Fading." yourlaunchproject.com, August 4, 2017.

Love, Remembered

Gilbert, Allison. *Passed and Present: Keeping Memories of Loved Ones Alive.* New York City: Seal Press, 2016

Kaplan, Louise J. *No Voice is Ever Wholly Lost.* New York City: Simon & Schuster; 1995.

Remembrance process.com

Roser, Laura A. *Your Meaning Legacy.* Yonker, NY: Golden Legacy Press, 2018.

ABOUT THE AUTHOR

Kathy Klaus is a lover of stories—everyday anecdotes, travel escapades and finding the funny wherever it lives. With a background in social work and the spirit of an entrepreneur, she attracts connection and seeks out innovation. She is energized by bright-eyed children, smiling golden retrievers and salmon fishing. Well traveled, her open mindedness has led to business ventures and personal adventures. Recently she received the designation of Certified Humor Professional from the Humor Academy, Association for Applied and Therapeutic Humor. Kathy lives in Alberta with her husband and enjoys regular visits to New York, sharing madcap activities with her grandchildren.